## DATE DUE

| | | | |
|---|---|---|---|
| OC 11 '96 | | | |
| DE 9 '96 | | | |
| AP 9 '97 | | | |
| NO 20 97 | | | |
| DE 16 97 | | | |
| MR 20 '98 | | | |
| N 23 99 | | | |
| MY 17 00 | | | |
| JE 1 0 00 | | | |
| NO 27 01 | | | |
| MY 22 03 | | | |
| JE 11 03 | | | |
| JY 15 04 | | | |
| DE 9 08 | | | |
| DE 13 09 | | | |

DEMCO 38-296

# *THE*
# RAINFORESTS
## *A CELEBRATION*

**LOBSTER CLAW** *(HELICONIA WAGNERIANA)*

(Gerry Ellis/Ellis Wildlife Collection)

# *THE*
# RAINFORESTS
## *A CELEBRATION*

COMPILED BY THE LIVING EARTH FOUNDATION
EDITED BY LISA SILCOCK

FOREWORD BY H.R.H. THE PRINCE OF WALES

OPPOSITE: BUTTRESS ROOTS IN RAINFOREST, COSTA RICA
(Michael & Patricia Fogden)

Chronicle Books · San Francisco

# The Rainforests

THE LIVING EARTH FOUNDATION is a registered UK environmental charity with education as the main focus of its work. Royalties from this book will go to a project in Cameroon, West Africa, whose aim is to work through schools to enable local communities to understand and value their precious environment and to manage their resources for the future. This is the first of what Living Earth intends will be a series of effective and innovative projects in tropical rainforest countries.

# FOREWORD

To walk in a tropical rainforest, as I was lucky enough to do on a recent visit to South America, is an intriguing experience. It is impossible not to feel awed by the beauty of the forest, by its immensity, by the sense of a history spanning millions of years. Giant trees stretch skywards, lifting their leaves a hundred feet or more to the light, their shallow roots supported by writhing buttresses. The air is moist, rich with the smell of rotting leaves.

Animals are hard to see in the dense forest vegetation, although you hear a veritable cacophony of hidden insects and birds. For me, one of the most memorable features was the number of stunningly beautiful butterflies which flitted across my path. Sounds are a clue to the rainforest, which is quite literally seething with life: worldwide, rainforests contain over half the species on earth.

But tropical rainforests are being destroyed at horrifying rates and on a scale that threatens us all. Species of plants are becoming extinct even before their potential benefits are known. When the rainforests go, water and soil are ruined, and the prospects for development and productive use of the land disappear. On a world scale, the possible effect on climatic stability could affect us all.

If only more people understood how economic prospects and potential for development are tied into the care and protection of natural resources, consumers and decision-makers might take different priorities when it comes to rainforests. There is no easy solution, but part of the answer must lie in education. Without education, efforts to protect the environment – rainforest or otherwise – are unlikely to gain the support necessary to enable them to succeed.

*The Rainforests: A Celebration*, besides being a celebration of these extraordinary ecosystems, also serves to build on the existing awareness and produce a deeper understanding of the role tropical rainforests play in the natural balance of our planet. It shows exactly what we stand to lose if this destruction continues and demonstrates why we must not allow this to happen. But the only way of preventing the destruction is if the developed world understands the costs involved. The developing countries have to be given assistance to achieve these aims.

In buying this book you also contribute directly to the future of rainforests. The Living Earth Foundation works for environmental education in Britain and elsewhere. The royalties from this book will go to support their project in Cameroon, which teaches schoolchildren living in and around rainforests about their environment. These children will form a new generation: one which, we hope, will know how to protect and manage its irreplaceable heritage.

# LIST OF CONTRIBUTORS

PROFESSOR GHILLEAN T. PRANCE is Director of the Royal Botanic Gardens, Kew. He was President of the Association of Tropical Botany (USA) in 1979/80 and of the American Society of Plant Taxonomists in 1984/5. He is currently President of the Systematics Association.

DR JULIAN CALDECOTT is a rainforest ecologist who has been involved in many projects concerning wildlife and forest conservation throughout South-East Asia. He is currently managing a major new national park in Nigeria.

DR TOM LOVEJOY, a tropical and conservation biologist, has worked in the Amazon forest of Brazil since 1965. From 1973 to 1987 he directed the programme of the World Wildlife Fund (US). In 1987 he was appointed Assistant Secretary for External Affairs at the Smithsonian Institution.

P. MICK RICHARDSON is currently a biochemical systematist at the New York Botanical Garden. He is author of a volume on hallucinogenic angiosperms and is writing a book on the evolution and ecology of toxic plants.

DR CAROLINE PANNELL holds a teaching post in the Department of Plant Sciences at the University of Oxford.

JONATHAN KINGDON is an evolutionary biologist, artist and author of numerous books and papers on mammals and visual communication in animals. He is now based in the Department of Zoology at the University of Oxford.

ANDREW MITCHELL is an author and zoologist who pioneered the use of lightweight aerial walkways to study the rainforest canopy. He is currently Marketing Director of Earthwatch.

PROFESSOR DAVID BELLAMY, botanist, writer and broadcaster was Senior Lecturer in botany at Durham University until 1982 when he founded the Conservation Foundation.

ROBIN HANBURY-TENISON is President of Survival International. In 1977-8, as one of Britain's leading explorers and travellers, he led 140 scientists to Borneo on the biggest expedition ever mounted by the Royal Geographical Society, which sparked off international concern for tropical rainforests.

ROGER HAMMOND is the Founder Director and Chief Executive of Living Earth.

LISA SILCOCK was assistant producer of the BAFTA Award winning film for Channel 4, *Baka – People of the Rainforest*. To make the film she lived with the Baka Pygmies in Cameroon, West Africa, for two years, learning to speak the language fluently. She is a freelance writer.

# CONTENTS

# INTRODUCTION
## Professor Ghillean T. Prance

T HIS BOOK IS CALLED **THE RAINFORESTS: A CELEBRATION.**
A strange title, perhaps, at a time when the forests' very
existence is threatened. What is there to celebrate, after all?
The media bombard us daily with the appalling facts and consequences of rainforest destruction; public concern has risen to
unprecedented levels; even politicians are embracing the issues.

The loss of the world's tropical rainforests is undoubtedly
one of the most serious crises we face today. But while many of
us can now quote horrifying statistics (an area the size of
Britain burned every year; a hundred or more species becoming extinct every day), we have only the haziest picture of what
the rainforests are and why they are so important. We understand the destruction; not what is actually being destroyed.

Once, rainforest covered the tropics to form an almost
continuous girdle around the earth, broken only by the sea and
odd areas of land whose climate was unsuitable. There are three
major rainforest regions: South and Central America, which
holds nearly three-fifths of the world's total; South East Asia,
and West and Central Africa. Smaller patches occur in Austra-
lasia, the Far East and the Indian sub-continent, as well as on
scattered islands throughout the tropics. But today, largely

---

BASILISK WAITING TO AMBUSH PASSING PREY IN TROPICAL RAINFOREST,

COSTA RICA

(Ken Preston-Mafham/Premaphotos)

through the activities of human beings, what used to be a thick carpet of virgin rainforest is now a broken mosaic; the ever dwindling areas of pristine forest are interspersed with many more which have been degraded, some slightly and some irrevocably; and some areas have long been completely devoid of trees.

It is estimated that half the world's tropical rainforests have already been lost; but this makes those that remain even more valuable. For rainforests are the oldest and richest expressions of life on our planet, and in a total area only the size of the United States support more than fifty per cent of all living species; plants and animals both beautiful and bizarre, uniquely adapted to the rainforests, most found nowhere else on earth. Many more are as yet undiscovered and unnamed, but could hold immense potential benefits for humanity. It is impossible not to feel a sense of wonder as we encounter the life of the rainforest: we see all that we are losing and realize that we cannot allow it to disappear like the rest, simply because we did not value it enough.

This book, therefore, celebrates the rainforests of the world: not only their considerable importance to human beings but the intricate web of life which is the essence of the forests themselves. Drawing from the accumulated wisdom of forest peoples and the skills of writers, scientists and photographers, the book shows some of the ways in which the rainforests actually work.

What, in fact, is a rainforest? The book outlines its requirements for growth and its basic life processes, and the evolutionary pressures which have, over millions of years, shaped these ecosystems into the most complex in the world and their inhabitants into the most varied and fantastic. We examine the extraordinary diversity of tropical rainforests, much touted but little understood, and the grave implications for the world if that diversity is lost. We build a picture of the rainforest as an interdependent community where neither animals nor plants can survive without the other, and all are part of an elaborate network of interactions which weaves through every part of the forest.

The entire rainforest community, which supports so much life, is held in a fine and delicate balance. As each component dies, its nutrients are recycled by a whole community of decomposing organisms and are then reabsorbed by the plants to provide new life for the forest. In the rainforests, this system of recycling has evolved over millions of years to become supremely efficient; it is only this which enables their poor soils to support a paradoxically luxuriant growth. The rich vegetation therefore gives a false impression of the soil's potential; for once the trees have gone, the land quickly becomes unproductive. Agriculturalists and cattle ranchers learn this to their cost, as the land they use gradually deteriorates. In the search for new, more fer-

**WATERFALL IN CLOUD FOREST, COSTA RICA**

(Michael Fogden/Bruce Coleman Ltd)

tile soils, they clear ever more forest land, contributing to the destruction already wreaked by development schemes and exploitation for timber and minerals.

It is sometimes hard to remember that human beings can live in and even exploit the forest without harming it, but we are reminded that it is indeed possible; traditional peoples have been doing so for centuries. They have accumulated a knowledge of and respect for their complex and finely balanced environment which is unequalled; but today, unable to resist the continuous onslaught to their lives and home, the forest people's plight is serious in the extreme. They are seeing the consequences of our disregard for their most fundamental principle: that you do not destroy the environment on which you depend.

Ultimately, we all depend on the rainforests, whether we realize it or not; yet if we do nothing, the rainforests will be gone in just forty years time. We will return to discuss this crisis at the end of the book; but first, let us enter into the threatened world of the rainforest, the richest natural treasure with which we share our planet.

# CHAPTER ONE

# THE RAINFOREST – AN OVERVIEW
## DR JULIAN CALDECOTT

*The rainforest is a living miracle of complexity, formed by more than half the species of animals and plants on earth – possibly many more. Although it supports millions of people directly, it and its products are also inextricably woven into our own lives, far away from the tropics. But as most of us are now aware, rainforests everywhere are being decimated, and with them, the life they support. There is no straightforward solution to this great threat; but though our knowledge of this most sophisticated of ecosystems is still very incomplete, the more we do understand of its complexity and fragility, the more we appreciate the imperative of protecting it. What, then, makes it so extraordinary; why must it be saved? What is this community of living things which we call rainforest?*

THE TROPICAL RAINFORESTS OF THE WORLD ARE ancient, complex ecosystems, teeming with diverse life forms. Here, there are soaring trees, their trunks often buttressed; a lofty canopy of branches and leaves, with deep shade below; climbing lianas and palms; plants growing on other plants; a rather bare forest floor, with lumpy roots writhing across it, a dusting of fallen leaves, and scattered ferns and seedlings. Butterflies dance in rare shafts of sunlight from above, birds make exotic noises, and insects sizzle and click.

This restless background is often overlaid by the rattling thunder of rain on distant leaves, and the dripping of water as it drains out of the canopy. The combination of warmth and rain makes the air of the forest very humid, often saturated with water vapour. Mists shroud the trees as sun succeeds storm,

---

1  SIERRA PALM FOREST, EL YUNQUE, PUERTO RICO
(Gerry Ellis/Ellis Wildlife Collection)

BETWEEN THE TROPICS OF CANCER AND CAPRICORN, FROM QUEENSLAND AND BORNEO TO BIAFRA AND YUCATAN OR AMAZONIA, WHERE THE TEMPERATURE IS HIGH AND CONSTANT AND THE ANNUAL RAINFALL IS MORE THAN 250MM/100IN, A DISTINCT TYPE OF FOREST GROWS. THESE ARE THE TROPICAL RAINFORESTS OF THE WORLD: ANCIENT, COMPLEX ECOSYSTEMS, TEEMING WITH DIVERSE LIFE FORMS, SHELTERING MORE THAN HALF THE SPECIES OF PLANTS AND ANIMALS ON EARTH – SOME BELIEVE MANY MORE. THEY COVER AN AREA ROUGHLY THE SIZE OF THE US – THREE-FIFTHS OF THIS IS IN CENTRAL AND SOUTH AMERICA. THEY ARE THE MOST THREATENED, IRREPLACEABLE AND VALUABLE ENVIRONMENTS IN THE WORLD.

rising up to form heavy clouds which pour out rain in their turn.

High temperatures and rainfall, more or less constant throughout the year, combine to produce the warm steamy atmosphere common to all the world's tropical rainforests, from Queensland to the Amazon basin. In these hothouse conditions, protected from cold and drought, plants and animals flourish in dazzling and as yet incalculable variety.

Paradoxically, one of the elements on which this teeming life depends also poses its greatest natural threat, and it is everywhere: dripping, trickling, prying into every crevice, water if left to its own devices would leach away all the forest's scarce and precious nutrients. Every organism in the forest is adapted to this perpetual battle against the insidious power of water. As a result, it has been estimated that only about one per cent of its total nutrients is eventually washed away by the rain.

Over the years, other adaptations have taken place; the longer a rainforest exists, the more intimate become the relationships between the multitudinous organisms of which it is composed. Over time, species adapt to one another: animals to plants, plants to animals, animals to animals, and plants to plants, each lineage refining its ecological 'niche' from generation to generation. This means that the requirements a species has for survival, and the ways in which it fulfils these needs, become more and more distinct over time. Animals and plants thus become increasingly successful survivors, ever more efficient exploiters or avoiders of exploitation. The tendency is for animals to get better and better at eating fewer and fewer things, for prey to protect themselves more and more rigorously, for plants to grow in increasingly special situations, and for particular species to make arrangements of mutual benefit with others - food and shelter, for example, exchanged for help in defence.

As species become more specialized, they leave room for others, and so give rise to new species with narrower ecological niches. As this occurs, the collective mass of species present in the environment becomes increasingly efficient at gathering, using and re-using essential nutrients. Members of species with very narrow ecological requirements do tend to be scarce, however. The reason for this is that they can only make use of resources (such as nutrients) which are in the particular form that they are adapted to exploit, and any such specific form will not be common; in addition, only a limited quantity of resources in any form is available in the forest at any one time. The outcome of all this is that in rainforests there are very many (mostly rare) species, living in very many curious and interdependent ways.

No other habitat on earth contains such a profusion or weight of plant life per hectare. Under the tropical sun, moreover, everything grows at astonishing speed. The rainforest produces new vegetable tissues faster than any other community on land. But death, too, is ever-present. A smell of decay hangs in the air and underfoot is a thin layer of debris. The forest's dynamism is fuelled by the speed of decay in the hot, damp, atmosphere, which acts as an incubator for scavenging and digesting organisms, and by the powerful flow of nutrient-carrying water from the ground to the canopy, drawn by the suction of evaporation from its myriad leaves. The rainforest is thus in dynamic balance, at a hectic rate of turnover.

It is the bright light of the tropical sun which powers the rainforest. Using solar energy, plants manufacture simple sugars from carbon dioxide in the atmosphere and from water, by the chemical process of photosynthesis. These sugars are the building-blocks of molecules which make up plants' cell walls and woody substance. Furthermore, they can be broken down as needed to provide energy and atoms for use in the complex biochemistry of life. They are used first by the plant that made them and subsequently, in one form or another, by organisms able to take them from the plant, or to retrieve them from its remains.

The structure of the rainforest is dictated by one overriding factor: almost all light is captured by the forest's canopy, casting the interior into deep shade. If a plant is to support itself by photosynthesis, it must therefore either be able to manage in semi-darkness, or it must somehow get its leaves into the canopy. A few plants are adapted to the shade of the rainforest floor, but they make up only a tiny portion of the forest's total flora. They include many ferns, the begonias, broad-leaved grasses and sedges, and gingers. More often to be seen in this twilight zone are small palms, bushes, seedlings and saplings, most of them destined one day, with luck, to reach the canopy as trees or lianas.

The rainforest is essentially a gallery whose monumental structure is made up of trees: their trunks provide its lower levels with a vertical framework, while the higher branches form a latticework roof. The tallest trees may be as much as sixty metres (200 feet) high, their trunks five metres (16 feet) in diameter near the ground, and often braced by woody buttresses like massive twisted fins. Trees of this size, known as 'emergents' are in a minority, however, and their crowns usually tower over those of their neighbours. Below them, the forest canopy becomes more continuous, the crowns of most adult trees standing shoulder to shoulder in a deep layer fifteen to forty-five metres (50-150 feet) above the forest floor.

This main level of the canopy is translucent, the light declining steadily in intensity as it filters through the leaves. This mass of vegetation offers opportunities for life to plants adapted to different and very specific degrees of illumination and, since the air within the forest is wetter than that outside, of moisture. Different tree species slot their adult crowns into the canopy at different heights depending on their physiological needs. Clinging to their branches and leaves, or to each other, are lesser plants which share their preferences – lichens and mosses, ferns and orchids in great and varied profusion. Interwoven within and draped across the canopy are the stems and foliage of climbing palms and lianas, which help to bind the forest into a continuous physical structure, and which often form a large part of the canopy itself.

In this intimidatingly diverse and dynamic environment, most of the action is hidden from view. Scientific documentation of the evolutionary relationships among the millions of rainforest species has only just begun, and many of the subtleties are only now starting to be explored. These include, for example, the ways in which 'arms races' between predators and their prey, herbivores and the plants they eat, can lead to chemical and behavioural defences of amazing power and complexity. They also include ways in which species manipulate others to achieve their own reproductive ends through pollination or seed dispersal.

But we are rapidly losing the chances of furthering this knowledge, and the wisdom that might flow from it, for we humans are sending a hundred or more rainforest species into extinction every day.

---

**2  FALLEN TREE IN CLOUD FOREST, VENEZUELA** (Stephen Dalton/OSF)
LIFE IN THE FOREST SILENTLY SEETHES WITH COMPETITION, SUCCESS AND
FAILURE. SOMETIMES, SOUNDS LIKE GREAT PISTOL SHOTS ECHO THROUGH THE
FOREST, FOLLOWED BY THE SPLINTERING, WHISTLING ROAR OF A FALLING TREE.
A GAP HAS BEEN RIPPED IN THE GREEN SHROUD OF THE FOREST, AND LIGHT
FLOODS IN TO ACTIVATE THE MANY SEEDLINGS OF THE FOREST FLOOR THAT
HAVE BEEN WAITING FOR JUST SUCH AN OPPORTUNITY FOR YEARS SINCE THEIR
HOPEFUL GERMINATION. A FURIOUS RACE BEGINS, AND LIFE FOAMS UPWARDS TO
CLOSE OUT THE SKY ONCE MORE. 'NATURAL FELLING' OF THIS KIND ACTUALLY
ENRICHES THE FOREST, ENCOURAGING COLONIZATION BY DIFFERENT SPECIES:
CONVERSELY, COMMERCIAL LOGGING CAN DAMAGE THE FOREST IRREVOCABLY.

5

3   CLOUDED RAINFOREST, CAPARAO NATIONAL PARK, SOUTH EASTERN BRAZIL.
(Luiz Claudio Marigo)

4 AND 5   MIST-SHROUDED RAINFOREST, BRAZIL, (C. S. Caldicott/Remote Source)
AND INDONESIA (Tony Stone Photo Library)
HEAT FROM THE TROPICAL SUN, WARMING THE ATMOSPHERE TO BETWEEN
17°-30°C 64°-86°F COMBINES WITH HEAVY RAINFALL TO PROVIDE A HOTHOUSE
AMBIENCE. PLANTS, WHICH FORM THE FRAMEWORK OF TROPICAL RAINFOREST.
THRIVE IN THE WARM, MOIST ATMOSPHERE: ANIMALS CAN RELAX THEIR GUARD
AGAINST COLD AND DROUGHT. CONDITIONS FOR GROWTH ARE IDEAL, BUT IT IS
PART OF THE NATURAL ECOSYSTEM THAT THERE ARE HIDDEN COSTS AND
HAZARDS FOR ALL THE RAINFOREST'S ABUNDANT LIFE.

**6 LOWLAND RAINFOREST, COSTA RICA** (Michael and Patricia Fogden) WATER AND SUNLIGHT PROVIDE NOT ONLY THE HOTHOUSE ATMOSPHERE WHICH SO FAVOURS PLANT GROWTH, BUT ALSO THE VERY BASES OF LIFE ITSELF. ALL LIVING THINGS, PLANT OR ANIMAL, ARE MADE UP OF COUNTLESS CELLS WHICH ARE FORMED LARGELY OF WATER. WATER, TOO, TRANSPORTS THE NUTRIENTS OF THE FOREST BETWEEN PLANTS AND WITHIN THEM; AND WATER PLUS SUNLIGHT POWERS THE RAINFOREST. SOLAR ENERGY ALLOWS THE PLANT TO MAKE SUGARS FROM CARBON DIOXIDE DRAWN FROM THE AIR, AND FROM WATER – A PROCESS KNOWN AS PHOTOSYNTHESIS. THESE SUGARS ARE THE BUILDING BLOCKS OF MOLECULES WHICH MAKE UP THE PLANT'S CELLS, AND PROVIDE THE ENERGY THEY NEED FOR GROWTH.

8

7   **TRAFALGAR FALLS, DOMINICA, WEST INDIES** (Gerry Ellis/Ellis Wildlife Collection)

8   **IGUASSA FALLS, BRAZIL/ARGENTINA** (Michael and Patricia Fogden)
WATER IS THE LIFE-BLOOD OF THE RAINFOREST, BUT THERE IS A HIDDEN COST
TO ITS ABUNDANCE HERE. THE WATER PRIES EVERYWHERE, DISSOLVING AND
ERODING, BREAKING THINGS UP AND SUCKING THEIR MOLECULAR REMAINS –
ESSENTIAL FOR THE FOREST'S NUTRITION – OUT OF THE FOREST, INTO RIVERS,
AND OUT TO SEA. THE WATER THREATENS THE SUBSTANCE OF THE FOREST
ITSELF, ITS TISSUES, MINERALS AND BIOCHEMICALS, ITS FOOD AND ITS VERY
STRUCTURE. BUT THE FOREST HAS ADAPTED TO THIS PRESSURE OVER THE
MILLENNIA: NUTRIENTS ARE STOLEN FROM BODIES LIVING AND DEAD, AND
CLAWED BACK FROM THE WATER BEFORE THEY ARE LOST FOR EVER. ALL OF THE
FOREST'S MANY LIVES ARE GEARED TO THIS PERPETUAL OBLIGATION.

9

9　MOSSMAN RIVER GORGE, QUEENSLAND, AUSTRALIA (Leo Meier/Weldon Trannies)

10　TREE FERNS, TORO NEGRO, PUERTO RICO
(Gerry Ellis/Ellis Wildlife Collection)
THERE IS A GREATER WEIGHT OF VEGETATION IN EACH HECTARE OF TROPICAL
RAINFOREST THAN THERE IS IN THE SAME AREA OF ANY OTHER HABITAT ON
EARTH. UNDER THE BRIGHT TROPICAL SUN, THE RAINFOREST PRODUCES NEW
VEGETABLE TISSUES FASTER THAN ANY OTHER COMMUNITY ON LAND. THIS HIGH
PRODUCTIVITY IS BALANCED AND SUSTAINED BY DEATH – AS MUCH TISSUE DIES
AS IS PRODUCED, ITS DECAY YIELDING NUTRIENTS FOR RE-USE. THE RAINFOREST
IS THUS IN DYNAMIC BALANCE, ITS RATE OF TURNOVER FRANTIC BY THE
STANDARDS OF OTHER FORESTS IN DRIER OR COOLER REGIONS. HOWEVER, THE
FINELY TUNED BALANCE OF THE RAINFOREST SYSTEM IS VERY VULNERABLE
ONCE DISTURBED.

11

12

**11 EMERGENT TREE, AMAZONIA**
(Tony Morrison/South American Pictures)

**12 EMERGENT TREE OVER CANOPY, KORUP NATIONAL PARK, CAMEROON** (Phil Agland)
TROPICAL RAINFOREST NATURALLY GROWS IN LOOSE 'TIERS' OF VEGETATION, WHICH RANGE IN HEIGHT FROM THE MINUTE TO THE MONUMENTAL. 55M/180FT OR MORE ABOVE THE GROUND, THE GIANT TREES OF THE RAINFOREST, THE EMERGENTS, THRUST INTO THE SUNLIGHT. BELOW THEM IS THE SPREADING SEA OF LEAVES KNOWN AS THE CANOPY, FORMED BY A DENSE LAYER OF TREES 15-30M/50-100FT DEEP. THE CANOPY FORMS THE BODY OF THE FOREST, AND IN TURN SHADES THE SHRUBS AND SMALL SAPLINGS BENEATH. THE SEEDLINGS, FERNS AND FUNGI COLONIZE THE FOREST FLOOR.

**13 SUNLIGHT, QUEENSLAND, AUSTRALIA** (Leo Meier/Weldon Trannies)
VERY LITTLE SUNLIGHT ACTUALLY REACHES THE FOREST FLOOR, EXCEPT THROUGH GAPS CREATED BY FALLEN TREES, OR THROUGH THE SPACES CREATED BY EMERGENTS PUSHING THROUGH THE CANOPY, AND THE ODD CHINK OPENED BY THE GENTLE MOVEMENT OF THE WIND IN THE MILLIONS OF LEAVES ABOVE. EVERY TREE, EVERY SAPLING, SHRUB AND SEEDLING, PUSHES UPWARDS TO THE SUN, SEEKING TO CAPTURE EVEN THE TINIEST RAY FROM THE SOURCE OF ITS LIFE AND ENERGY.

13

15

**14  RAINFOREST TREE, QUEENSLAND, AUSTRALIA** (Leo Meier/Weldon Trannies)
EVOLVED OVER MILLENNIA, AND OFTEN HUNDREDS OF YEARS OLD, RAINFOREST
TREES ARE FAR FROM BEING THE PASSIVE ORGANISMS THEY APPEAR. TREES SUCK
NUTRIENTS AND WATER FROM THE SOIL, AND ABSORB CARBON DIOXIDE FROM
THE ATMOSPHERE AND SUNLIGHT THROUGH THEIR LEAVES. TREES MUST FLOWER
AND ATTRACT POLLINATORS IN ORDER TO REPRODUCE; THEY MUST PRODUCE
FRUIT WHICH IS TEMPTING TO THE CREATURES WHO WILL DISPERSE THEIR SEEDS
TO ALL THE CORNERS OF THE FOREST AND ENSURE THE SURVIVAL OF THE
SPECIES. TREES MUST DEFEND THEMSELVES AGAINST PREDATORS, PARASITES
AND DISEASE PRODUCING ORGANISMS, AND TREES ARE THE FRAMEWORK OF THE
FOREST, THE STRUCTURE ON WHICH ALL OTHER LIFE RESTS: WITHOUT THE TREES
THE REST OF THE COMMUNITY CANNOT SURVIVE.

**15  BUTTRESS ROOTS OF FOREST FIG TREE, SABAH, MALAYSIA**
(Gerald Cubitt/Bruce Coleman Ltd)
THE ROOTS OF TREES SUCK UP ESSENTIAL NUTRIENTS AND MOISTURE FROM THE
SOIL, BUT THEY ALSO ANCHOR THE TREE SECURELY IN THE GROUND. HOWEVER,
THE ROOTS OF RAINFOREST TREES ARE OFTEN VERY NEAR THE SOIL SURFACE,
PERHAPS BECAUSE THIS IS WHERE THE GREATEST CONCENTRATION OF RICH
NUTRIENTS LIES. THESE SURFACE ROOTS MAY SUPPORT MONUMENTAL
STRUCTURES, OFTEN OVER 55M/180FT TALL, WHOSE WOOD IS HARD AND HEAVY –
THE PRIZE OF THE TROPICAL TIMBER TRADE. THE TREES' ENORMOUS BULK IS
STABILIZED BY BUTTRESS ROOTS, WHICH SPREAD THE WEIGHT OVER A WIDER AREA.

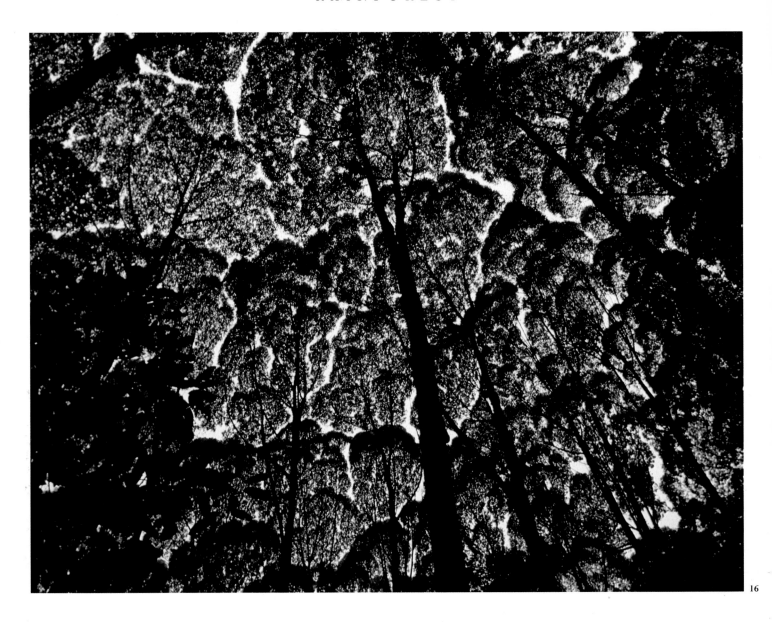

16

**16 RAINFOREST CANOPY FROM BELOW, MALAYSIA** (Earl of Cranbrook)
THE TREES OF THE CANOPY DO NOT TOUCH ONE ANOTHER, BUT NEATLY
INTERLOCK. THE REASON FOR THIS IS UNKNOWN – IT MAY BE TO PREVENT THE
SPREAD OF DISEASE, OR TO MAKE ACCESS FROM ONE TREE TO ANOTHER
DIFFICULT FOR PREDATORS. BUT TO ALL INTENTS AND PURPOSES THE CANOPY
FORMS A CLOSED LAYER, SHUTTING OUT THE SUN AND SHUTTING IN THE
MOISTURE. BELOW THE INSULATION OF THE CANOPY, THERE IS LITTLE SUNLIGHT
AND LITTLE WIND: TEMPERATURE AND HUMIDITY REMAIN MORE OR LESS EVEN,
DAY OR NIGHT, AND THE FOREST AIR IS BOTH COOLER AND MOISTER THAN
ABOVE THE TREES. WITHOUT THE CANOPY COVER AND THE WATER-RETAINING
PROPERTIES OF THE ROOTS OF THE FOREST PLANTS, THIS LUSH AND APPARENTLY
FERTILE GROUND IS QUICKLY AND IRREVOCABLY TURNED TO DESERT.

**17 CLIMBING FIG, BRAZIL** (Ken Preston-Mafham/Premaphotos)

**18 *VICTORIA REGIA* LILIES, AMAZONIA, BRAZIL** (C. S. Caldicott/Remote Source)
RAINFOREST PLANTS GROW IN A HUGE VARIETY OF WAYS: CLINGING, CLIMBING,
FLOATING, AND TWISTING THROUGH THE TREES. THE DIVERSITY OF PLANTS IN
THE RAINFOREST IS A SIGN OF ITS GREAT AGE. OVER MILLIONS OF YEARS THE
LIFE OF THE FOREST HAS EVOLVED INTO MANY FORMS WITH ENDLESS
REFINEMENTS FOR EXISTENCE IN A SPECIALISED ENVIRONMENT. THE RESULT IS
AN EXTRAORDINARY ARRAY OF DIVERSE SPECIES, MANY OF WHICH ARE NOW
BECOMING EXTINCT BEFORE THEY ARE EVEN DISCOVERED.

17

18

19

**19  EYELASH VIPER ON PALM, COSTA RICA**

(Michael and Patricia Fogden)

THIS EYELASH VIPER IS STRICTLY TREE-DWELLING; LIKE ALL RAINFOREST CREATURES, IT HAS ITS OWN CLEARLY DEFINED NICHE WITHIN THE ECOSYSTEM. THE SNAKE IS ALSO COMPLETELY DEPENDENT ON ITS ENVIRONMENT: IT IS ADAPTED TO FEED ON RAINFOREST PREY, SURVIVE IN RAINFOREST CLIMATE, AND HAS EVOLVED TECHNIQUES OF HUNTING AND HIDING ONLY WITHIN THE RAINFOREST CONTEXT. IF IT LOSES THIS FRAMEWORK, THE SNAKE, LIKE COUNTLESS OTHER ANIMALS AND PLANTS, WOULD BE UNABLE TO ADAPT TO THE SUDDEN CHANGE AND WOULD FACE CERTAIN EXTINCTION AS A SPECIES.

**20  AERIAL ROOTS OF A FIG TREE, CAIRNS, AUSTRALIA** (Weldon Trannies)

**21  VARZÉA FLOODED FOREST, BRAZIL** (Luiz Claudio Marigo)
WITHIN THE DIVERSE AND DYNAMIC ENVIRONMENT WHICH IS THE RAINFOREST,
MOST OF THE ACTION IS HIDDEN FROM VIEW. IT IS IMPOSSIBLE TO SAY HOW
MANY SPECIES OF PLANTS AND ANIMALS ARE CONTAINED IN THE VARZÉA
FLOODED FOREST, OR HOW MANY ARE SUPPORTED BY THE ABUNDANT FRUITS OF
THE FIG TREE. SCIENTIFIC STUDY OF THE LIFE OF THE RAINFOREST HAS ONLY
JUST BEGUN. SUCH RESEARCH OFFERS POTENTIALLY ENORMOUS REWARDS: BUT
WILL THE RAINFORESTS OF THE WORLD SURVIVE LONG ENOUGH FOR US TO
COMPLETE IT?

CHAPTER TWO

# INFINITE VARIETY – A RICH DIVERSITY OF LIFE
## Dr Tom Lovejoy

*Tropical rainforests hold the greatest diversity of life of any environment on earth. Hidden by the vegetation from all but the trained eye are a multitude of plants and animals, rare, strange and beautiful. Among them are many species as yet undiscovered and unnamed, which may be of immense potential value to humanity; and there exist in the rainforest life forms which occur nowhere else in the world. What are the reasons for this extraordinary diversity of life, which we are in the process of eliminating before we even know its full extent?*

T HE NUMBERS ARE ASTONISHING. THE AMAZON, WHICH drains the world's largest tropical rainforest, is thought to have about 3000 species of fish, including fruit-eating fish and the electric eel. This is more than are contained in the entire North Atlantic. The tropical forest country of Panama has 1500 species of butterfly, compared with 763 in the United States and a mere 68 in Great Britain. There are more species of woody plant on a single volcano in the Philippines than in the entire United States. Five times as many kinds of tree grow on the island of Madagascar as in the whole of temperate North America. The list is endless.

Given this bewildering and exhilarating variety, it is to the shame of modern science – and it is also perhaps its greatest critical challenge – that, while it has constructed devices with the potential to destroy civilization and most of biological diversity, it has failed so far to discover even to within an order of

---

22 CARNIVOROUS PITCHER PLANTS, MALAYSIA

(Gerald Cubitt/Bruce Coleman Ltd)

IT USED TO BE SAID THAT TROPICAL RAINFORESTS CONTAINED SOME HALF OF THE TOTAL NUMBER OF THE WORLD'S SPECIES. BUT IN THE LAST TWENTY YEARS, THE ESTIMATE OF THAT TOTAL NUMBER OF SPECIES HAS RISEN FROM THREE MILLION TO SIXTY MILLION. THE STUDIES WHICH HAVE LED TO THIS HUGELY INCREASED STATISTIC HAVE ALMOST ALL BEEN OF RAINFOREST LIFE. SOME SCIENTISTS NOW BELIEVE THAT THE TROPICAL RAINFORESTS OF THE WORLD MAY HOLD UP TO NINETY PER CENT OF THE PLANT AND ANIMAL SPECIES ON EARTH.

magnitude how many species there are in the world. It has neglected the basic inventory of life on earth at the very time when a great deal of it may be lost.

About one and a half million species of plants and animals have been described, of which one million are from the temperate zone. But it has been estimated that there remain some sixty million undescribed. Twenty years ago the total was put at a mere three million. Almost all the rise in this estimate is due directly to work in the tropical rainforests. The work of Terry Erwin on insects of the Amazon forest canopy, in particular, has suggested that biologists have considerably underestimated the amount of diversity. It used to be thought that half of all the world's species were contained in the tropical forests that occupy just seven per cent of the earth's dry land surface. Now many scientists believe that as much as ninety per cent of all plant and animal species are to be found there.

If counting the number of species is perhaps the simplest and most practical way of estimating this diversity, we should remember that there are countless further sub-divisions that this system does not take into account of. A discussion of the dog family in these terms, for instance, would consider only the thirty-five or so species into which the family can be divided, disregarding the many different breeds of domestic dog, let alone the genetic differences that allow us to recognize the family hound with such certainty.

Even at a local level the diversity of rainforests is remarkable. Whereas a temperate forest might have ten or fifteen species of tree, and in extreme cases maybe as many as thirty, tropical forests have hundreds of tree species. In one ten-hectare (25-acre) plot in the central Amazon, researchers have identified over 300 species of tree. A recent study in Malaysia recorded 835 species of tree in fifty hectares (125 acres). It has been estimated that a typical patch of rainforest just six kilometres (four miles) square contains as many as 1500 species of flowering plant, 750 species of tree, 400 species of bird, 150 species of butterfly, 100 species of reptile and 60 species of amphibian. The numbers of insects are so great that they can only be guessed at, but one hectare (2½ acres) may contain as many as 42,000 species. Tropical forests, therefore, represent the most biologically diverse communities and are the most complex systems known in the universe.

When considering the protection of biological diversity it is not enough just to protect the full array of plant and animal species. It is important as well to protect the different assemblages of species that make for distinct biological communities. Recent studies of butterflies in three one-hectare (2½-acre) plots in the central Amazon, for example, recorded 217 of 454 species known in the general area. However, even though the three plots were close to one another and superficially appeared to be similar forest, only about twenty-five per cent of the butterfly species were shared in common by the three plots, and twenty-five per cent were unique to each plot.

It is likely that as many as ninety per cent of the species of the tropical forests remain to be discovered and described, quite apart from any understanding of their distribution. This makes assessing conservation priorities extremely difficult. The need for an inventory of biological diversity in the tropical forests in time for conservation action to be effective is clearly very urgent. In the meantime, one dependable strategy for conservation is to protect forests which are recognizably different: in that way it is fairly certain that a broad range of variously adapted animals and plants will also be conserved.

As many as forty different types of rainforest have been distinguished, falling into four main categories. The first, tropical evergreen lowland forest, forms two-thirds of what we call rainforest; it has the greatest species diversity and the most luxuriant growth; then there is inundated forest, with small and stunted trees; thirdly, tropical moist deciduous forest, which is somewhat seasonal and contains trees which shed their leaves; and finally montane forest, including cloud forest, which gains much of its moisture from the surrounding mist.

Forest types are classified first by non-biological factors such as total rainfall, temperature, altitude and seasonality (primarily of rain); this system has the advantage of being applicable to any country, without reference to flora and fauna, and will identify basic types of ecological communities. These parameters can be further refined to include such factors as true seasonality and soil type, and will thus identify further forest types; even narrower classifications are possible if one adds forests that are so dominated by one kind of woody plant they can be recognised from the air, such as the various bamboo and palm forests. Further variation is correlated with geography. Roughly speaking, the forests of Zaire, Madagascar, Central America and Indonesia are likely to have no species in common at all. But more importantly, even the Atlantic forest of Brazil shows considerable difference in species distribution from the Amazon, as do adjacent valleys of the Andes, and the islands in the Philippines or Indonesia.

All this is significant because scientists believe that isolation is the primary factor in the evolution of new species. If a species is divided by an accident of geography or geology into two isolated populations of sufficient size, each will develop separately. This could occur on isolated islands, or in forest interrupted by a different type of growth, as in the case of the two Brazilian forests. If enough time elapses, members of the two populations will be so distinct that they will be unable to interbreed if once more brought into contact with one another, and one species will have become two new ones.

In certain parts of the rainforest, particularly in West Africa and Amazonia, studies of the distribution of well-known groups of organisms such as birds, butterflies and frogs have shown special areas where there are clusters of species which occur only in a limited range. These are thought by many to represent places where isolated patches of forest managed to survive in a succession of cool dry periods during the northern continents' Ice Age. In these areas, known as refuges, new species evolved. While this theory, which may help explain the origin of so much diversity in these forests, remains a hypothesis, it is beyond dispute that these areas contain species which occur nowhere else and hence should be priorities for conservation.

When the world's forests are being destroyed at a rate of close to forty hectares (100 acres) per minute, it is obviously important to act according to conservation priorities which already exist. Yet unless our knowledge of the flora and fauna of the tropical forests is increased rapidly and systematically, a great deal of biological diversity will slip through our fingers – and with it an incalculable reservoir of potential knowledge. In the field of medical science alone, the rainforests have yielded drugs effective against Hodgkin's disease, leukaemia and malaria, among many others.

The list of useful products of all sorts that derive from the forests is infinite, and new ones are being identified all the time. There is, moreover, the extraordinary potential of the dawning age of genetic engineering, a science that does not make new genes (contrary to myth), but depends on rearrangements of the existing ones. From this perspective, the ultimate wealth of the tropical nations is the genetic stock of their forests, from which incalculable and inconceivable benefits may be derived.

It is impossible to over-estimate the importance of the knowledge that stands to be lost with the biological diversity of these forests. For each species represents a unique combination of traits, each one of which is an evolutionary solution to biological problems. With each species lost, the potential growth of the life sciences is forever curtailed and impoverished. If we permit the loss of the rainforests, and with them a major portion of biological diversity, it might with justice be viewed as one of the greatest acts of desecration in human history.

---

23  ANGWANTIBO, WEST CENTRAL AFRICA (Phil Agland/Partridge Films)
THE RAINFOREST CAN BE SEEN AS A MOSAIC OF DIFFERENT MICRO-
ENVIRONMENTS WHICH MAKE UP THE GREATER WHOLE. THESE MICRO-
ENVIRONMENTS ARE CREATED BY DIFFERENT GROUPINGS OF VEGETATION, BY
THE HEIGHT OF THE HABITAT FROM THE GROUND (FOR INSTANCE, WHETHER
CANOPY OR SHRUB LAYER), BY AVAILABLE LIGHT, SOIL TYPE AND WETNESS. MOST
ANIMALS STAY FIRMLY WITHIN ONE OF THESE ENVIRONMENTS AND DO NOT
VENTURE INTO OTHERS: THUS MANY MONKEYS ALMOST NEVER DESCEND TO THE
GROUND, WHEREAS CERTAIN BIRDS NEVER GO HIGHER THAN THE SHRUB LAYER.
THIS HELPS TO REDUCE COMPETITION WITH OTHER SPECIES WHICH MAY HAVE
SIMILAR REQUIREMENTS; SO WHILE THE INSECT-EATING ANGWANTIBO OCCUPIES
THE LOW SHRUB LAYER OF THE FOREST, THE POTTO, ANOTHER PRIMATE WHICH
EATS INSECTS AND FRUITS, LIVES IN THE FOREST CANOPY. THE TWO WILL NEVER
NEED TO VIE FOR FOOD.

24 MONTANE FOREST, EASTERN
ANDES (Tony Morrison/South American
Pictures)

RAINFOREST IS A GENERIC TERM
ENCOMPASSING A WIDE RANGE OF
FOREST TYPES. THEY ARE
CLASSIFIED ACCORDING TO
FACTORS SUCH AS SOIL TYPE,
SEASONALITY, AND ALTITUDE INTO
AS MANY AS FORTY FOREST
FORMATIONS. BECAUSE
KNOWLEDGE OF THE SPECIES
WITHIN RAINFORESTS IS STILL SO
LIMITED, THIS CLASSIFICATION IS
USEFUL FOR CONSERVATION
PURPOSES. IF A CROSS-SECTION OF
FOREST TYPES WERE PRESERVED,
THIS WOULD ENSURE THAT THEIR
VARIOUS INHABITANTS WOULD
ALSO SURVIVE. THE TERM
'MONTANE' INCLUDES SEVERAL
FURTHER FOREST TYPES, SUCH AS
ELFIN, WHERE THE TREES ARE
STUNTED AND TWISTED BY HIGH
WINDS, AND CLOUD FOREST,
WHERE THE ALTITUDE IS SUCH
THAT CLOUD ENCIRCLES THE
TREES IN SWIRLING MIST AND THE
HUMIDITY IS VERY HIGH.

**25  BUTTRESS ROOTS AND LIANAS, LOWLAND RAINFOREST, PERU**
(Michael and Patricia Fogden)
THE WORD 'RAINFOREST' IS GENERALLY UNDERSTOOD TO MEAN THE LOWLAND
OR LOW MONTANE TYPE, SUCH AS IS FOUND IN THE AMAZON BASIN, IN WEST
CENTRAL AFRICA, AND IN PARTS OF SOUTH EAST ASIA. IT IS THIS FOREST WHICH
HAS THE GREATEST SPECIES DIVERSITY, IS LEAST SEASONAL AND HAS MAINLY
EVERGREEN GROWTH. HOWEVER, THIS SHOULD NOT BE TAKEN TO MEAN THAT
LOWLAND IS THE ONLY KIND OF RAINFOREST WORTHY OF NOTE OR STUDY – AND
IT CERTAINLY SHOULD NOT BE IMAGINED THAT IT IS THE ONLY RAINFOREST TYPE
WHICH IS UNDER THREAT.

**26   FLOODED GALLERY FOREST, VENEZUELA**

(Sullivan & Rogers/Bruce Coleman Ltd)

THE GALLERY FORESTS ARE CORRIDORS OF RAINFOREST-LIKE GROWTH
BORDERING RIVERS WHICH FLOW THROUGH OTHERWISE NON-RAINFOREST
REGIONS. THIS LUXURIANT GROWTH MAY BE ONLY A FEW KILOMETRES WIDE
FROM THE RIVER TO ITS GRASSLAND EDGE, BUT STILL HARBOURS MANY OF THE
SPECIES FOUND IN THE NEARBY AMAZON BASIN. GALLERY FOREST, LIKE SOME
AUSTRALIAN RAINFOREST, SOME BRAZILIAN ATLANTIC COAST REGIONS AND SOME
FORESTS ELSEWHERE IN SOUTH AMERICA, TENDS TO BE STRONGLY SEASONAL.
UNLIKE SOME RAINFORESTS WHICH HAVE HEAVY RAINFALL ALMOST ALL THE
YEAR, THESE FORESTS HAVE A DISTINCT DRY SEASON, DURING WHICH THE
DECIDUOUS TREES, OF WHICH THERE ARE MANY, DROP THEIR LEAVES.

**27   GIANT TREE FERNS, ATLANTIC
FOREST, SOUTHERN BRAZIL**
(Claudio Marigo)

THE ATLANTIC RAINFOREST OF
COASTAL BRAZIL IS QUITE DISTINCT
FROM THAT OF THE BRAZILIAN
AMAZON. SEPARATED BY NON-
RAINFOREST TERRAIN, THE TWO
FORESTS HAVE EVOLVED
INDEPENDENTLY WITH ONLY A
LIMITED OVERLAP OF SPECIES.
TREE FERNS FAVOUR VERY WET
FOREST AND NEED PLENTY OF
LIGHT, PIONEERING GROWTH IN
THE GAPS CREATED BY FALLEN
TREES. THEY CAN REACH 20M/65FT
IN HEIGHT. THERE ARE AT LEAST
700 SPECIES OF TREE FERN
THROUGHOUT THE TROPICS AND
SUBTROPICS, SOME GROWING IN
ONLY A VERY LIMITED RANGE.
HUGE CHUNKS OF BRAZIL'S
ATLANTIC RAINFOREST HAVE BEEN
CLEARED FOR CATTLE RANCHING
AND IT IS NOW IN IMMINENT
DANGER OF EXTINCTION.

28

**28 SLOW LORIS, MALAYSIA** (Gerald Cubitt/Bruce Coleman Ltd)
IT IS RARE FOR TWO KINDS OF ANIMAL IN ONE FOREST TO HAVE EXACTLY THE
SAME NEEDS IN ONE FOREST – TO OCCUPY THE SAME ECOLOGICAL 'NICHE'. A
'NICHE' IS THE ANIMAL'S SLOT IN THE ECOSYSTEM: WHAT IT EATS, WHERE IT
LIVES IN THE FOREST, WHAT PREYS ON IT, AND SO ON. EQUIVALENT NICHES SEEM
TO EXIST IN GEOGRAPHICALLY SEPARATE RAINFORESTS, BUT CAN BE OCCUPIED
BY ONE SPECIES IN AFRICA AND QUITE ANOTHER IN THE AMERICAS. HOWEVER,
THE ANIMALS EVOLVE PHYSICALLY TO EXPLOIT THESE NICHES AND TEND TO
LOOK ALIKE: COMPARE THIS LORIS WITH THE UNRELATED AFRICAN ANGWANTIBO
ON PAGE 39.

**29  TAMANDUA ANTEATER,
AMAZON BASIN, PERU**
(Michael and Patricia Fogden)

**30  GIANT PANGOLIN, SOUTH
EASTERN CAMEROON**
(Lisa Silcock/Dja River Films)
THE SOUTH AMERICAN TAMANDUA
AND THE AFRICAN PANGOLIN
ILLUSTRATE THE WAY THAT
DIFFERENT SPECIES WITH SIMILAR
REQUIREMENTS TEND TO EVOLVE
THE SAME PHYSICAL
CHARACTERISTICS WHICH BEST
SUIT THEIR LIFE-STYLE. THIS
THEORY IS KNOWN AS
CONVERGENT EVOLUTION. THUS
BOTH ANIMALS, WHICH SPECIALIZE
IN EATING ANTS AND TERMITES
(THE GIANT PANGOLIN CAN
CONSUME 200,000 ANTS A NIGHT,
WEIGHING SOME 700G/1½LB), HAVE
EVOLVED NARROW HEADS,
TOOTHLESS MOUTHS AND LONG,

NARROW, STICKY TONGUES WITH
WHICH TO PROBE THE NESTS OF
ANTS AND TERMITES, AND MASSIVE
CLAWS FOR DIGGING COMPACTED
MOUNDS. BOTH PANGOLIN AND
ANTEATER ARE ENDANGERED:
PANGOLIN MEAT IS PRIZED, WHILE
TAMUNDUAS ARE KILLED ON
ROADS IN DEVELOPED AREAS OR
FOR SPORT; AND CERTAIN
ANTEATER SPECIES ARE COLLECTED
FOR THE LIVE ANIMAL TRADE. BUT
DESTRUCTION OF THEIR HABITAT
MAY PROVE AN EVEN GREATER
THREAT.

30

31

32

33

31  **FAN PALM LEAVES** (Simon Bracken/Weldon Trannies)

32  **RAINFOREST HERB LAYER, COSTA RICA** (Michael Fogden/Bruce Coleman Ltd)

33  **HELICONIA LEAVES, MONTEVERDE, COSTA RICA** (Michael Fogden/Bruce Coleman Ltd)
THE DIVERSITY OF RAINFOREST PLANT LIFE IS STAGGERING: IN A TYPICAL PATCH
OF RAINFOREST JUST 6.5KM/4 MILES SQUARE, THERE CAN BE AS MANY AS 1500
SPECIES OF FLOWERING PLANT AND 750 SPECIES OF TREE. IN THE MONTEVERDE
FOREST AREA OF COSTA RICA, WHERE TWO OF THESE PICTURES WERE TAKEN,
THERE ARE AN ESTIMATED 2500 SPECIES OF PLANT. COMPARE THE FIGURES FOR A
10-HECTARE/25-ACRE PLOT OF TEMPERATE FOREST, WHICH MIGHT YIELD FIFTEEN
OR, AT MOST, THIRTY TREE SPECIES: AN EQUIVALENT AREA OF AMAZON
RAINFOREST CONTAINS SOME 300. MANY OF THESE PLANTS HAVE NOT EVEN BEEN
NAMED, AND ALMOST NONE HAVE BEEN INVESTIGATED SCIENTIFICALLY. GIVEN
THAT OVER FORTY PER CENT OF DRUGS PRESCRIBED IN THE US OWE THEIR
POTENCY TO 'NATURAL' CHEMICALS, MAINLY FROM RAINFOREST PLANTS, HOW
MANY POSSIBLY REVOLUTIONARY DRUGS COULD WE BE LOSING DAY BY DAY
WITH EACH HECTARE OF RAINFOREST?

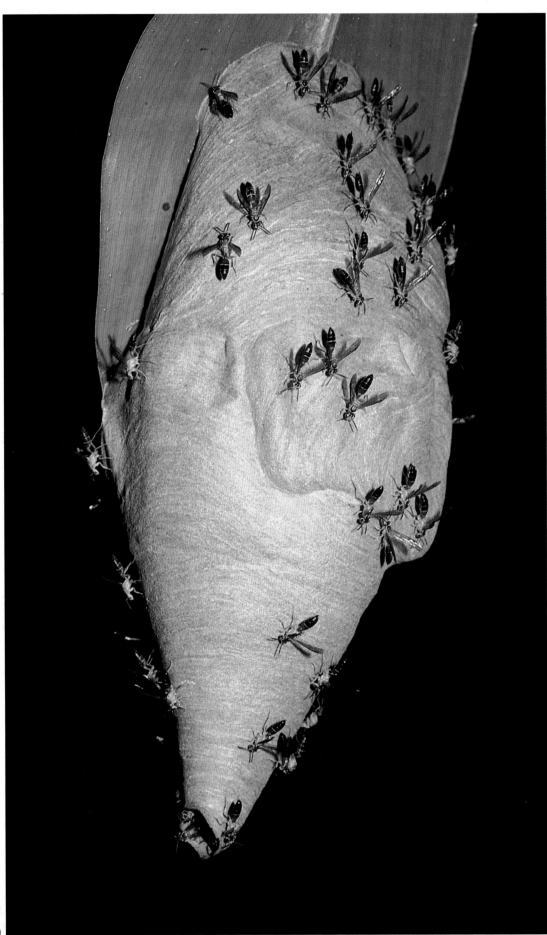

**34 SOCIAL WASPS, TRINIDAD**
(Ken Preston-Mafham/Premaphotos)
THESE COMMON RAINFOREST WASPS ARE ONE OF A HUGE RANGE OF TROPICAL FOREST SPECIES. THEIR NESTS, WHICH ARE CONSTRUCTED LIKE THOSE OF EUROPEAN WASPS FROM WOOD SCRAPINGS, ARE SUSPENDED UNDER BROAD LEAVES TO PROVIDE SHELTER. FROM THIS PROTECTED POSITION THE WASPS ARE QUICK TO SWARM OUT OF THE ENTRANCE TO THE NEST AT THE SLIGHTEST DISTURBANCE AND INTO DEFENSIVE POSTURE, ABDOMENS ERECT, READY TO STING. THIS STRATEGY AND THEIR PAINFUL STINGS MAKE THEM A RARE PREY: THEIR ONLY SERIOUS ENEMIES ARE THE COLONIES OF ARMY ANTS RAMPAGING THROUGH THE FOREST. AN ARMY ANT RAID WILL CLEAN THE NEST OF EGGS, LARVAE, FOOD STORES AND ANY WASP UNABLE TO ESCAPE. THE REST OF THE COLONY SWARM NEARBY, HELPLESS IN THE FACE OF THE PLUNDERERS.

**35 ARMY ANTS CARRYING WASP LARVA, COSTA RICA**
(Michael and Patricia Fogden)
ARMY ANTS ARE FAMOUS FOR THEIR SPECTACULAR PREDATORY RAIDS. THE COLONIES OF SOME SPECIES CAN NUMBER UP TO TWO MILLION, WHILE IN AFRICA THE SIMILAR DRIVER ANT COLONIES MAY NUMBER TWENTY MILLION. THESE CARNIVOROUS ANTS FORAGE MAINLY ON THE FOREST FLOOR, WHERE THEY PIN DOWN AND CARRY OFF ANY INSECT TOO TARDY TO MOVE AWAY FROM THE ENDLESS COLUMN WHICH CAN NUMBER UP TO 50,000 INDIVIDUALS. ANTS HAVE A HIGHLY DEVELOPED SOCIAL ORDER IN WHICH EACH CASTE, WHETHER QUEEN, WORKER OR SOLDIER, HAS ITS OWN SPECIFIC ROLE, AND IN EVOLUTIONARY TERMS THEY ARE HIGHLY SUCCESSFUL INSECTS. THERE ARE LITERALLY THOUSANDS OF SPECIES OF ANTS IN THE WORLD'S TROPICAL RAINFORESTS; THEY HAVE COLONIZED EVERY PART OF IT FROM FLOOR TO CANOPY.

34

35

**36 EGGS OF RAIN FROG LAID ON MOSS, COSTA RICA**

(Michael Fogden/OSF)

OF THE MANY FROGS WHICH LIVE AT ALL LEVELS OF THE CENTRAL AND SOUTH AMERICAN RAINFORESTS, THE RAIN FROGS ARE THE MOST COMMON. REMARKABLY, RAIN FROGS NOT ONLY LAY THEIR EGGS ON LAND, BUT UNDERGO THE ENTIRE METAMORPHOSIS FROM EGG TO FULLY FORMED FROG OUT OF WATER, EACH FROGLET FINALLY EMERGING A TINY 6MM/¼IN LONG. THIS TERRESTRIAL LIFECYCLE IS ONLY POSSIBLE IN THE HUMID ATMOSPHERE OF THE RAINFOREST, WHERE THE EGGS, AND FROG, WILL NOT DRY OUT.

36

**37 GOLDEN TOADS, MONTEVERDE CLOUD FOREST, COSTA RICA**

(Michael and Patricia Fogden)

THESE BEAUTIFUL GOLDEN TOADS ARE EXTREMELY RARE. THEY ARE ENDEMIC TO THE MONTEVERDE CLOUD FOREST, AND OCCUR ONLY WITHIN AN AREA OF 500M/550YDS BY 5KM//3 MILES. THEY WERE FIRST DISCOVERED JUST FIFTEEN YEARS AGO, TO THE DISBELIEF OF THE BIOLOGIST, WHO THOUGHT THEY HAD BEEN DYED. IN THE LAST TWO YEARS ONLY ONE INDIVIDUAL HAS BEEN SIGHTED: OBVIOUSLY, SUCH RARE SPECIES ARE EXTREMELY VULNERABLE. POPULATIONS CAN PROBABLY RECOVER FROM NATURALLY CAUSED PROBLEMS, BUT IF THEIR HABITAT WERE NOT PROTECTED THE TOADS COULD BE IN SERIOUS DANGER OF EXTINCTION.

37

**38  SHIELD BUGS, AUSTRALIA**

(Ken Preston-Mafham/Premaphotos)
THE EXTRAVAGANT COLOURS OF
THESE SHIELD BUGS ARE AN
INDICATION TO HOPEFUL
PREDATORS THAT THEY ARE
EITHER TOXIC OR DISTASTEFUL – A
SURVIVAL STRATEGY EMPLOYED BY
MANY ANIMALS, PARTICULARLY
INSECTS, IN SOME CASES AS A
BLUFF BY HARMLESS ONES.
GROUPING TOGETHER OF SUCH
INSECTS IS COMMON, AND HAS THE
FUNCTION FIRSTLY OF
INTENSIFYING THE WARNING
MESSAGE, AND SECONDLY OF
DETERRING PREDATORS. AN
INEXPERIENCED PREDATOR,
SAMPLING ONE INSECT, WOULD
NOT VENTURE TO TRY ANOTHER,
THUS PROTECTING THE REST OF
THE GROUP WHO ARE ALL FROM
THE SAME PARENTS. THE GENES
AND BY FAR THE MAJORITY OF THE
KIN, ARE SAFE.

38

**39  TENT BATS UNDER LEAF, COSTA
RICA** (Michael and Patricia Fogden)
BATS OF ALL SHAPES AND SIZES
MAKE UP A LARGE PROPORTION OF
RAINFOREST MAMMAL SPECIES – UP
TO 50% – AND ACCOUNT LARGELY
FOR THEIR DIVERSITY. THESE TINY
FRUIT-EATING 'TENT' BATS ARE
ABOUT 50MM/2IN LONG AND ARE
ONE OF THE VERY FEW SPECIES
WHICH ARE ALMOST ENTIRELY
WHITE. THE 'TENT' IS CREATED BY
THE BATS NIBBLING DOWN EITHER
SIDE OF THE MIDRIB OF A LARGE
HELICONIA LEAF: THE LEAF
DROOPS ON EITHER SIDE,
PROVIDING SHELTER. LIKE A
SULTAN IN HIS SERAGLID, EACH
MALE TENT BAT ROOSTS WITH A
HAREM OF FEMALES, WHICH IN
THIS CASE NUMBERS ABOUT
TWENTY.

39

**40 THORN BUGS, SOUTH AMERICA**
(Ken Preston-Mafham/Premaphotos)
THORN BUGS, SO NAMED BECAUSE
OF THEIR DISGUISING CARAPACE,
ARE COMMON, IN A GREAT RANGE
OF DIFFERENT HABITATS, FROM
BRAZIL TO SOUTH FLORIDA: THERE
ARE OVER THIRTY SPECIES IN
COSTA RICA ALONE. THESE THORN
BUGS HAVE EVOLVED THE IDEAL
CAMOUFLAGE TO ENSURE THEIR
SURVIVAL: FROM AFAR THEY
RESEMBLE THORNS, BUT FROM
CLOSE TO THEY HAVE DISCREET
WARNING COLORATION, WHICH
WILL ALERT AN INTERESTED
PREDATOR TO THEIR
UNPALATABILITY. THEIR SHAPE
ALSO PROBABLY MAKES THEM AN
ANGULAR AND UNCOMFORTABLE
MOUTHFUL FOR A BIRD.

40

41

AT LEAST HALF THE WORLD'S 8,500
SPECIES OF BIRDS LIVE IN
TROPICAL RAINFOREST. AFTER
INSECTS, BIRDS ARE THE GREATEST
EXPRESSION OF THE DIVERSITY OF
THE FOREST, OCCUPYING EVERY
AVAILABLE NICHE IN THE SYSTEM.
IN TROPICAL FOREST, BIRDS OF
SEVERAL DIFFERENT SPECIES WILL
FORAGE THROUGH THE FOREST
TOGETHER IN PARTIES FOR
MUTUAL BENEFIT. THUS INSECT-
EATING BIRDS WILL CLUSTER
AROUND FRUIT-EATERS, WHOSE
PECKING DISTURBS THE INSECTS. A
GREATER NUMBER OF INDIVIDUALS
ALSO GIVES BETTER PROTECTION
AGAINST PREDATORS.

42

41   RED-NECKED TANAGER
(Luiz Claudio Marigo)

42   SEVEN-COLOURED TANAGER
(Luiz Claudio Marigo)
THERE ARE HUNDREDS OF SPECIES
OF TANAGER THROUGHOUT THE
NEW WORLD - 220 EXIST IN SOUTH
AMERICA ALONE – AND BY FAR THE
MAJORITY HAVE THEIR HOME IN
TROPICAL RAINFORESTS.
EXTRAVAGANTLY COLOURED,
MAINLY FRUIT-EATING BIRDS,
TANAGERS TEND TO HAVE NARROW
ECOLOGICAL NICHES. DIFFERENT
SPECIES LIVE AT DIFFERENT
ALTITUDES: THEIR NUMBERS
INDICATE THE DIVERSITY OF
HABITATS WHICH EXIST WITHIN
THE RAINFOREST. THEIR NEED FOR
SPECIFIC ENVIRONMENTS MEANS
THAT MANY SPECIES CAN LIVE IN
CLOSE PROXIMITY WITHOUT
HAVING TO COMPETE FOR FOOD.

43

**43   GREEN HONEY CREEPER**
(Luiz Claudio Marigo)
THE HONEY CREEPER IS PART OF
THE TANAGER FAMILY, THOUGH IT
SEEMS TO BE MORE ADAPTABLE
THAN THE TANAGERS THEMSELVES:
IT CAN LIVE IN BOTH PRISTINE
TROPICAL FOREST AND SECONDARY
GROWTH, AND IT FORAGES FOR
FOOD IN A RANGE OF HABITATS,
FROM THE LOWER LEVELS OF THE
FOREST TO THE TREE TOPS, EITHER
ALONE OR IN GROUPS.

**44   LOTEN'S SUNBIRD (MALE), SRI
LANKA**
(Dieter and Mary Plage/Bruce Coleman Ltd)
THE SUNBIRD OCCUPIES THE SAME
ECOLOGICAL NICHE IN THE OLD
WORLD AS THE HUMMINGBIRD IN
CENTRAL AND SOUTH AMERICA,
AND RANGES FROM AFRICA TO
ASIA. LIKE THE HUMMINGBIRDS,
THEY ARE TINY, OFTEN
IRIDESCENT, JEWEL-LIKE DRINKERS
OF NECTAR, BUT THE TWO GROUPS
ARE NOT AT ALL RELATED.

**45  PIERID BUTTERFLY LAYING
EGGS, COSTA RICA**
(Michael and Patricia Fogden)
A PATCH OF RAINFOREST JUST
6.5KM/4 MILES SQUARE CAN HOLD
150 DIFFERENT KINDS OF
BUTTERFLY, THOUGH GIVEN THE
COMPOSITE NATURE OF THE
FOREST ENVIRONMENT,
COMMUNITIES OF ONE BUTTERFLY
SPECIES MAY STAY IN ONE PATCH
OF FOREST AND NOT VENTURE
INTO ANOTHER WHICH IS
OCCUPIED BY A DIFFERENT
SPECIES. A STUDY IN THE AMAZON
OF THREE NEIGHBOURING ONE-
HECTARE/TWO-AND-A-HALF-ACRE
PLOTS REVEALED THAT ONLY
ABOUT TWENTY-FIVE PER CENT OF
BUTTERFLY SPECIES WERE SHARED
IN COMMON BY THE THREE AREAS.

**46  CAT-EYED SNAKE EATING EGGS
OF RED-EYED LEAF FROG, COSTA
RICA** (Michael and Patricia Fogden)
THE CAT-EYED SNAKE IS A
SPECIALIZED KILLER: A PREDATOR
OF FROGS' EGGS, IT WILL HUNT ALL
NIGHT AMONG THE LEAVES AND
PLANT-FORMED POOLS OF THE
CANOPY FOR ITS FOOD. FROGS
ENSURE THE SURVIVAL OF THEIR
SPECIES BY VARIOUS MEANS
INCLUDING LAYING LARGE
NUMBERS OF EGGS, SOME OF
WHICH WILL SURVIVE.

46

47

**47   BRACONID WASP PUPAE ON PARASITIZED CATERPILLAR**
(Michael Fogden/Bruce Coleman Ltd)
PARASITISM PLAYS A SIGNIFICANT ROLE IN THE RAINFOREST ECOSYSTEM, AND
INVOLVES MANY SPECIES WHICH CAN ONLY REPRODUCE BY USING – AND OFTEN
ULTIMATELY KILLING – ANOTHER LIVING ORGANISM. THE PARASITES ARE
SOMETIMES SO SPECIALIZED THAT ONLY ONE SPECIFIC PLANT OR ANIMAL CAN
ACT AS THE HOST. THE FEMALE BRACONID WASP LAYS HER EGGS ON THE
CATERPILLAR: THE LARVAE DEVOUR ONLY THE NON-ESSENTIAL PART OF THE
CATERPILLAR, WHICH THEREFORE TAKES SOME TIME TO DIE, AN UNWILLING
FOSTER PARENT TO THE BROOD OF WASPS WHICH EVENTUALLY HATCH.

**48 GOLDEN BEETLE, CLOUD FOREST, COSTA RICA**
(Michael and Patricia Fogden)
IT IS NOT KNOWN HOW MANY BEETLE SPECIES EXIST IN THE RAINFOREST, BUT THE NUMBER IS WITHOUT DOUBT PHENOMENAL. BEETLES ACCOUNT FOR THE LARGEST PROPORTION OF ANIMAL DIVERSITY IN THE RAINFOREST: SO FAR ONLY A COMPARATIVELY FEW SPECIES HAVE BEEN ENUMERATED. EVEN A REMOTELY ACCURATE ESTIMATE MIGHT GIVE US A CLUE TO THE REAL LEVEL OF SPECIES DIVERSITY IN THIS UNCHARTED ENVIRONMENT.

**49 FEMALE MARSUPIAL FROG, CLOUD FOREST, VENEZUELA**
(Michael and Patricia Fogden)
THE FEMALE MARSUPIAL FROG LAYS HER EGGS, WHICH ARE THEN FERTILIZED BY THE MALE WHO INSERTS THEM INTO A SAC ON HER BACK. THIS SEALS OVER, CREATING A MOIST AND PROTECTED ENVIRONMENT IN WHICH THE EGGS CAN MATURE. AFTER SOME FOUR WEEKS THE SEETHING, WRIGGLING, FULLY FORMED FROGLETS EMERGE. THIRTY-TWO FROGLETS CAME OUT OF THE SAC OF THIS FEMALE.

48

49

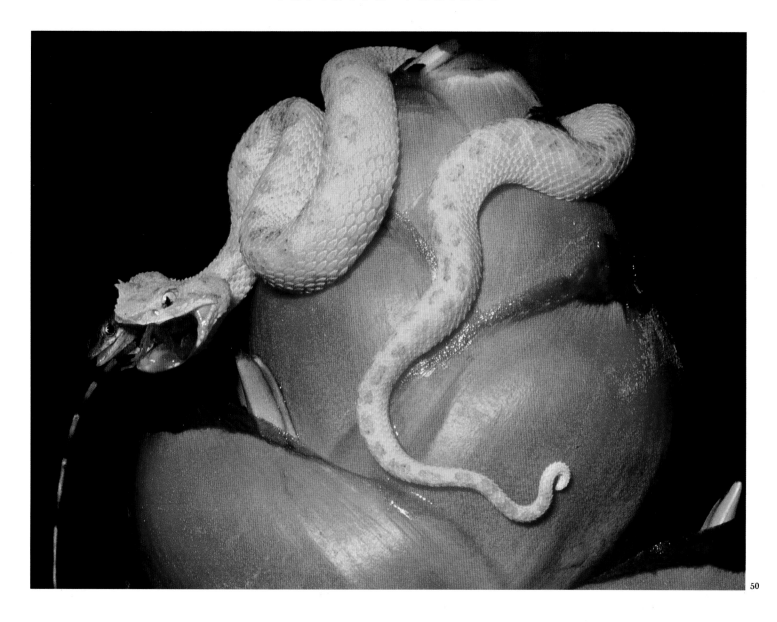

50

**50 EYELASH VIPER KILLING ANOLE ON HELICONIA FLOWER, COSTA RICA**

(Michael and Patricia Fogden)

THE EYELASH VIPER OCCURS IN A VARIETY OF COLOURS, THE MOST SPECTACULAR BEING THIS GOLDEN YELLOW. IT USES ITS COLOUR AS A LURE; SMALL BIRDS, FOR INSTANCE, ARE ATTRACTED BY THE BRIGHTNESS; BUT AN INVESTIGATION OF IT MAY PROVE FATAL. SPECIALIZED KILLERS, VENOMOUS SNAKES LIKE THE VIPERS ARE AMONG THE MANY RAINFOREST PLANTS AND ANIMALS WHICH USE POISON BOTH TO DEFEND THEMSELVES AND TO HUNT.

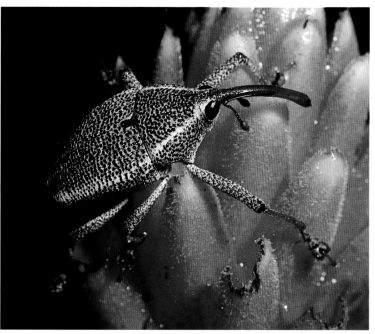

51

**51 WEEVIL ON GINGER FLOWER, COSTA RICA**

(Ken Preston-Mafham/Premaphotos)

WEEVILS, CHARACTERIZED BY THEIR LONG SNOUTS, ARE COMMON IN RAINFORESTS THROUGHOUT THE TROPICS. WEEVILS BORE THEIR SNOUTS INTO THE FLESHY PARTS OF SEEDS AND PLANTS TO FEED; THE HOLE ALSO MAKES A SAFE DEPOSIT FOR THE FEMALE'S EGGS.

53

**52   LAR GIBBON AND YOUNG, SOUTH EAST ASIA** (Rod Williams/Bruce Coleman Ltd)

**53   BLACK HOWLER MONKEY, SOUTH AMERICA** (Rod Williams/Bruce Coleman Ltd)
MONKEYS ARE AT THEIR MOST DIVERSE IN TROPICAL RAINFORESTS, AND ARE ·
SUPREME EXPLOITERS OF THEIR ARBOREAL ENVIRONMENT. THE HOWLER
MONKEY ALMOST NEVER DESCENDS BELOW THE MIDDLE STOREY OF THE
FOREST, WHILE THE LAR GIBBON, LIKE THE OTHER GIBBONS, IS AMONG THE
FASTEST OF ALL FOREST ANIMALS THROUGH THE TREE-TOPS. PERFECTLY
ADAPTED, THEY CAN ACHIEVE GREAT SPEEDS AS THEY SWING ARM TO ARM
THROUGH THE CANOPY OF TREES, SOMETIMES LEAPING 15M/ALMOST 50 FEET AT A
TIME.

# CHAPTER THREE

# THE TROPICAL ARMS RACE –
# STRATEGIES FOR SURVIVAL
## P. Mick Richardson

*The rainforest is not merely a random collection of plants and animals but a highly complex interactive community. Trees provide the framework for this community, supporting it in a huge variety of ways. Throughout the rainforest ecosystem, however, there is continual conflict between species, and no conflict has shaped the forest so profoundly as the evolutionary battle between the trees and the herbivores. Their war has been fought with chemicals, and has been played out through the millennia in tropical forests all over the world.*

THE TREES AND OTHER RAINFOREST PLANTS, WHICH build themselves almost from thin air, forming organic compounds from sunlight, atmospheric carbon dioxide and water, constitute the first link in the food chain. They are thus the primary requirement of life for the next link in the chain: the huge numbers of plant-eating insects and other herbivores in the forest. Finding themselves in the front line of the battle for survival, these plants are faced with a dilemma. For at the same time as needing to attract beneficial pollinators and seed dispersers, they must also minimize the damage caused by the

54 CATERPILLARS OF LYCAENID BUTTERFLY FEEDING ON CYCAD LEAF, COSTA RICA (Michael and Patricia Fogden)

THE GREATEST POTENTIAL THREAT TO THE HEALTH OF THE FOREST IS POSED BY THE HERBIVORES: UNTRAMMELLED, THEY WOULD DECIMATE EVERY PLANT. HOWEVER, OVER THE MILLENNIA THE RAINFOREST PLANTS HAVE EVOLVED DEFENCES BOTH STRUCTURAL AND CHEMICAL: IN MANY TREES, EVERY LEAF, ROOT, FRUIT AND FLOWER, THE BARK AND THE WOOD ARE PROTECTED BY A POISONOUS OR DISTASTEFUL COMPOUND. BUT THEIR PREDATORS HAVE RESPONDED. SUCCESSIVE GENERATIONS HAVE ADAPTED TO DEAL WITH THE DEFENCES, PROVOKING ONGOING 'CHEMICAL WARFARE' BETWEEN PLANT AND PREDATOR. AS A RESULT ANIMALS HAVE EVOLVED WHICH SPECIALIZE IN FEEDING ON ONLY ONE OR TWO KINDS OF PLANT THAT WOULD BE DEADLY TO OTHERS. ONLY THE CATERPILLARS SHOWN HERE, ALONG WITH ONE BEETLE SPECIES, ARE ABLE TO EAT THE LEAVES OF THIS HIGHLY TOXIC CYCAD. THE CATERPILLARS ACTUALLY SYNTHESIZE THE INGESTED LEAF POISONS AND USE THEM FOR THEIR OWN DEFENCE: THEIR COLOURATION WARNS POTENTIAL PREDATORS THAT THEY ARE DANGEROUS.

marauding army of forest herbivores. Without some form of protection the trees would be stripped bare and smaller plants completely devastated: but over millions of years these seemingly passive organisms have evolved a number of ingenious defences which ensure their survival and, by extension, that of the forest.

Few forest trees produce new leaves continuously throughout the year. Young growing leaves are especially vulnerable; but plants can safeguard them to some degree either by producing leaves in the dry season when insects are few in number, or by producing synchronized flushes of leaves which will satiate the herbivore population. They may even do both, by producing a flush of leaves at the end of the dry season.

As the leaves mature they become tougher and more resistant to insect attack. Some plants shield their leaves with a thick, waxy cuticle; others have evolved forms of physical defence, such as thorns or spines, while the trunks of many forest trees, including palms and the ginseng family, have a dense armour of sharp spines to prevent larger animals reaching their leaves, flowers and fruits. The vast majority of plants, however, lack these visible forms of defence: they are protected by various types of chemical compounds, which course through every part of them.

These chemical defences take a huge variety of forms, and are remarkably effective. The leaves of some plants, for instance, have stinging hairs which cause an immediate and severe burning sensation on the skin. Others, especially of the sumac family, contain chemicals that can cause an allergic reaction in the intestines of a herbivore which is strong enough to deter it from trying the plant again. Yet other leaves contain substances which, while harmless themselves, are phototoxic, reacting with ultraviolet light to form poisonous compounds which disable or kill the unfortunate predator. However, most of the protective chemical compounds used by plants merely taste unpleasant, deterring predators at first bite – though they may have a cumulative poisonous effect if the animal continues to eat the plant.

Lethal poisons may be used in this struggle for survival: some plants contain cyanogenic glycosides which, when the cells are disrupted by a predator's bite, liberate hydrogen cyanide (prussic acid), a toxin which inhibits respiration. The seed coats of the castor oil plant contain one of the most toxic substances known to humanity, a protein called ricin, of which a single molecule is enough to kill an entire cell.

Many of these defensive chemicals are familiar to us – strychnine and cyanide, for example, are common in rainforest plants. Others contain bitter tannins, which we know through the astringent taste they impart to unripe fruit or dry red wine. Every group of plants tends to specialize in the production of a particular set of chemical compounds; trees of different species growing side by side in the forest may contain completely different defensive chemicals, so that a herbivore which can safely eat the leaves of one tree may be poisoned by its neighbour. In this way, plants have contrived not only individual defence mechanisms, but also a communal one, for it is impossible for a single predator to devastate even a small area of forest.

In the relentlessly competitive environment of the forest, however, such ingenuity does not go unchallenged: it appears that a sort of chemical 'arms race' is being fought by the plants and their insect predators. In response to the chemicals which the plant produces to deter them, the insects evolve detoxification mechanisms or other means of overcoming the protective poisons. The plants, in turn, now evolve new chemical defences. In time the insects' remarkable adaptive abilities will overcome these too, and so the escalation continues. The results of this unresolved war are ever more specialized relationships between insects and plants. Fewer and fewer predators are able to feed on any one species of tree, and each predator may feed on an increasingly limited number of host plants.

Some fascinating examples of interdependence have developed as a result of this co-evolution of plants and their insect predators. Butterfly larvae which feed on plants in the carrot family containing phototoxic chemicals avoid danger by feeding at night, further protecting themselves by spending the daylight hours wrapped in a curled leaf, which acts as a shield against ultraviolet light. Most insects are believed to deal with chemical compounds by detoxifying and excreting them, but in apparently increasing numbers they are learning to store the chemicals in their bodies in order to make themselves toxic to their predators. Aphids which feed on plants in the Asclepiadaceae family, for instance, store cardenolide substances which have psychoactive properties, causing the spiders which eat them to spin disrupted webs.

Many such poisonous insects are brightly coloured as if to advertise their toxicity, with, for instance, the vivid pigments of carotenoid substances which are obtained from the host plant during feeding. Other insects also have ways of exploiting the poisons intended to deter them: male danaid butterflies, for example, seek out pyrrolizidine alkaloids from the crotolaria plant and modify them for use as aphrodisiacs during courtship.

A large number of plants, including the well-known rubber plant, resort simply to gumming up the mouthparts of their predators. When damaged they produce latex, which oxidizes on exposure to air to form a viscous glue. Needless to say, among their insect predators there are some which have contrived to bypass this threat: biting through the plant's major veins, they drain the latex, interrupting its flow to their intended feeding sites, an ingenious ploy also used by some insects on leaves which contain poisonous chemicals.

Some plants protect themselves with cunning molecular

trickery. Many plants in the legume family, for instance, produce amino acids which, though different, are structurally similar to the amino acids found in proteins. More than 1200 legumes, for example, are known to contain canavanine, a non-protein amino acid that is related to the protein amino acid, arginine. Most insects, on eating the plant, will incorporate the wrong amino acid into their proteins in place of arginine; the aberrant proteins do not function correctly, and as a result the insects die. The bruchid beetle, however, uses the seed of one such plant, *Dioclea megacarpa* which contains almost thirteen per cent canavanine, as a nursery. The larvae feed on the seeds with impunity, because they manufacture a protein-building enzyme which can discriminate between canavanine and arginine. With breathtaking aplomb, the beetle also metabolizes the canavanine for use as food.

More extraordinary still are the plant compounds which interfere with the very life cycles of their predators. Insects often go through a complex series of larval and adult stages and several moults, which are controlled by juvenile and moulting hormones, before reaching maturity. Some plants contain large amounts of the juvenile hormone of predatory insects, causing them to remain in the larval stage and ultimately to die without reproducing. Others do the opposite, producing substances which overcome the effects of juvenile hormones, with the result that the insects skip some vital larval stages and become precocious and imperfect adults, while yet others contain compounds which interfere with the moulting process. A similar technique is used to deter mammalian herbivores by a group of plants containing substances which imitate the effects of oestrogen, thus lowering their fertility rates.

The defensive compounds produced by plants are, by definition, potent substances. Only a very few from rainforest plants have been investigated for their useful potential, but of those that have, the results have been impressive. Plants produce fungicides, insect repellents, and also pesticides to deter predators: some have been found which, unlike many synthetic chemicals, are effective against insects but harmless to mammals. One of the most obvious examples, rubber, evolved by the plant to protect itself, is of great economic importance to many tropical countries and has never been matched by synthetics. Defensive chemicals are the active ingredients in practically all plant-derived medicines, which currently make up forty per cent of the drugs prescribed in the West. The compounds evolved by rainforest plants which make them so successful could, by judicious breeding and genetic manipulation, be used to strengthen the resistance of food plants to disease and predators in areas of the world where people are struggling to grow food. The list of possible benefits is endless. If we allow the rainforests to survive, we could tap their wealth, established over millions of years of evolutionary warfare, for many years to come.

**55 TINY GRASSHOPPER NYMPHS
CLUSTERED ON LEAF, MALAYSIA**
(Ken Preston-Mafham/Premaphotos)
GRASSHOPPERS OF ALL SPECIES
CAN WREAK HAVOC IN THE FOREST.
SOME ARE ONLY ABLE TO FEED ON
A FEW PLANTS WHILST OTHERS
SEEM ABLE TO DEAL WITH A WIDE
VARIETY OF LEAVES. THESE
NYMPHS WILL MOULT SEVERAL
TIMES BEFORE THEY ARE FULLY
GROWN, AND WHEN ADULT WILL
BE WARNINGLY COLOURED,
SUGGESTING THAT THEY MAY
STORE TOXIC LEAF COMPOUNDS.

57

**56   YOUNG LEAVES OF CERCROPIA TREE, SOUTH AMERICA**
(Tony Morrison/South American Pictures)

**57   MAIDENHAIR FERN, TRINIDAD** (Ken Preston-Mafham/Premaphotos)
YOUNG LEAVES ARE PARTICULARLY VULNERABLE TO PREDATORS, AS IT IS OFTEN
SOME TIME BEFORE THEY TOUGHEN AND DEVELOP THEIR DEFENSIVE
COMPOUNDS. RED PIGMENTATION IS COMMON IN YOUNG LEAVES; IN THE
CANOPY, THE PIGMENT MAY BE A PROTECTION AGAINST THE HARSH RAYS OF THE
SUN. ITS CHEMICAL BASE, ANTHOCYANIN, ALSO FORMS THE BUILDING-BLOCKS
FOR THE DEFENSIVE COMPOUNDS WHICH DEVELOP AS THE LEAF MATURES.

59

**59 FLAG BUG ON PASSION FLOWER, TRINIDAD** (Ken Preston-Mafham/Premaphotos)
THESE BUGS SUCK THE SAP OF THE FLOWER, BUT HAVE EVOLVED TO COPE WITH
THE POISONOUS COMPOUNDS IT CONTAINS. LIKE MANY OTHER INSECTS, THE
FLAG BUG STORES THE TOXINS AND ADVERTISES ITS PRESENCE TO PREDATORS
WITH VIVID WARNING COLOURATION.

**58 PASSION FLOWER, SOUTH AMERICA** (Nick Gordon)
ALL FLOWERS SUFFER THE DILEMMA OF NEEDING TO ATTRACT POLLINATORS
WHILE RESISTING PREDATORS. PRIMARILY IN RESPONSE TO THE HELICONID
BUTTERFLIES AND LARVAE, THEIR PRIMARY PREDATORS, THE PASSION FLOWERS
HAVE EVOLVED AN EXTRAORDINARY RANGE OF DEFENCES. SOME LURE ANTS
WITH ABUNDANT NECTAR, THE INSECTS ACTING AS STINGING GUARDIANS
AGAINST PREDATORS; OTHERS HAVE BARBED STEMS WHICH WILL IMPALE A
CLIMBING CATERPILLAR; STILL OTHERS HAVE DEVELOPED YELLOW BLOBS TO
MIMIC BUTTERFLY EGGS, DETERRING THE FEMALE BUTTERFLY FROM LAYING A
REAL BATCH; AND FINALLY, MOST PARTS OF PASSION FLOWERS ARE INEDIBLE –
THOUGH NOT THE NECTAR, WHICH IS THE POLLINATOR'S PRIZE.

60

**60 MOUNTAIN GORILLA, RWANDA**
(R.I.M. Campbell/Bruce Coleman Ltd)
GORILLAS EAT VAST QUANTITIES OF
VEGETABLE MATTER, INCLUDING
LEAVES, ROOTS, BARK AND FRUITS.
HOWEVER, UNLIKE INSECTS, WHICH
HAVE LIMITED INTELLIGENCE AND
MOBILITY, GORILLAS CAN BOTH
MAKE CHOICES OF FEEDING
MATTER AND MOVE AROUND TO
SELECT THE CHOICEST LEAVES, SO
THEY DO NOT NEED TO EVOLVE TO
FEED SPECIFICALLY ON ONE
SPECIES OF LEAF. ALTHOUGH IT
HAS ALMOST NO ANIMAL
PREDATORS, EXTENSIVE POACHING
NOW MEANS THAT THE MOUNTAIN
GORILLA IS GREATLY
ENDANGERED.

61

**61 GOLDEN BAMBOO LEMUR
EATING BAMBOO, MADAGASCAR**
Ken Preston-Mafham/Premaphotos)
VERY FEW ANIMALS WILL EAT ANY
BUT THE YOUNGEST AND MOST
DELICATE SHOOTS OF BAMBOO, AS
THE OLDER LEAVES ARE WELL
DEFENDED WITH TOXIC
COMPOUNDS. HOWEVER, THIS RARE
LEMUR HAS A SPECIALLY ADAPTED
DIGESTIVE SYSTEM TO COPE WITH
THE POISONS CONTAINED IN THE
PLANT.

62

**62 COLLARED PECCARY CENTRAL AMERICA,** (Partridge Films)
PECCARIES ARE MAJOR PREDATORS OF SEEDS IN THE FOREST, AND HAVE
EVOLVED EXTREMELY POWERFUL JAWS CAPABLE OF CRACKING THE HARDEST
SHELLS. PECCARIES AND RODENTS SUCH AS THE AGOUTIS, ACCOUNT FOR THE
LOSS OF MANY SEEDS AND ALSO SEEDLINGS. PLANTS COUNTER THESE
PREDATORS WITH A NUMBER OF STRATEGIES, FROM PRODUCING SO MANY SEEDS
THAT SOME ESCAPE BEING EATEN, OR PRODUCING TINY SEEDS WHICH PROVIDE
LITTLE FOOD AND SO ARE NOT TEMPTING, TO PROTECTING THEIR SEEDS BY
CHEMICAL MEANS.

**63  LIMACODIDAE MOTH LARVAE, VENEZUELA** (Ken Preston-Mafham Premaphotos)
CATERPILLARS, WHICH ARE SOFT AND SLOW MOVING, OFTEN STAYING ON THE
SAME LEAF FOR LONG PERIODS OF TIME, ARE POTENTIALLY EXTREMELY
VULNERABLE TO PREDATORS. BUT MANY OF THEM HAVE EVOLVED DEFENCES
WHICH DETER ALL BUT THE MOST INEXPERIENCED OF ANIMALS. THE
LIMACODIDAE MAY WARN OF THEIR VERY PAINFULLY STINGING HAIRS WITH
THEIR BRIGHT GREEN 'COATS', THOUGH GREEN IS NOT USUALLY A WARNING
COLOUR.

**64 BUTTERFLY CATERPILLAR, CAMEROON**
(Michael Fogden/Bruce Coleman Ltd))

**65 LIMACODIDAE MOTH LARVA, JAVA** (Ken Preston-Mafham/Premaphotos)

**66 NYMPHALIDAE BUTTERFLY LARVA, MALAYSIA**
(Ken Preston-Mafham/Premaphotos)
MANY CATERPILLARS HAVE STINGING SPINES, WHICH EVEN TO A HUMAN CAN CAUSE SPORADIC ITCHING FOR UP TO A YEAR. THESE SPINES, WHICH IN SOME CASES TRAIL ONTO THE LEAF, BLUR ITS OUTLINE AND HENCE THE SHADOW WHICH MIGHT OTHERWISE GIVE IT AWAY. ALTHOUGH THE CATERPILLARS' BASIC COLOURS ARE CRYPTIC (MOSTLY GREEN TO MERGE WITH THE LEAVES ON WHICH THEY FEED), ON CLOSER INSPECTION A PREDATOR WOULD BE ALERTED TO DISCREET WARNING COLORATION, SUCH AS THE YELLOW AND BLACK BELT, AND THE YELLOW-TIPPED SPINES.

68

69

**67 BUTTERFLY CHRYSALIS, CENTRAL AMERICA** (Partridge Films) THE CATERPILLAR SPENDS ITS ENTIRE LARVAL STAGE EATING AND GROWING, PREPARATORY TO PUPATING. SUSPENDED FROM A LEAF OR BRANCH, THE CHRYSALIS DEVELOPS IN WHICH THE METAMORPHOSIS FROM CATERPILLAR TO BUTTERFLY OR MOTH TAKES PLACE. WHEN THE ADULT FINALLY EMERGES, IT WILL NO LONGER EAT LEAVES BUT IT IS THOUGHT THAT SOME CATERPILLARS WHICH FEED ON TOXIC PLANTS AND STORE POISONS FOR THEIR OWN PROTECTION MAY MAINTAIN THESE DEFENCES THROUGH METAMORPHOSIS, THUS CONFERRING THEM ON THE NEW BUTTERFLY OR MOTH.

**68 SWALLOWTAIL BUTTERFLY LARVA MIMICKING BIRD DROPPING, PANAMA** (Ken Preston-Mafham/Premaphotos) LIKE MANY RAINFOREST CREATURES, SOME CATERPILLARS CHOOSE DISGUISE AS A DEFENCE AGAINST PREDATORS, RATHER THAN STINGING SPINES OR TOXIC COMPOUNDS. THIS LARVA, GIVING NO CLUE TO THE SPECTACULAR BUTTERFLY IT WILL BECOME, INNOCUOUSLY IMITATES A BIRD DROPPING.

**69 MOTH LARVA, BOLIVIA** (G.I. Bernard/NHPA) THE HAIRS ON THIS ENCLEIDAE MOTH CATERPILLAR CAN INFLICT A VICIOUS STING ON THE UNWARY – ANIMAL OR HUMAN.

70

70   UNIDENTIFIED FLOWER,
MONTANE FOREST, AMAZON/ANDES
(Tony Morrison/South American Pictures)

71   **RAIN ON LEAVES, JAVA**
(Alain Compost/Bruce Coleman Ltd)
AS WELL AS DEFENDING
THEMSELVES FROM PREDATORS,
RAINFOREST PLANTS MUST GUARD
AGAINST THE WATER WHICH IS
EVERYWHERE. WATER POOLING ON
THE LEAF COULD ENCOURAGE THE
FORMATION OF ALGAL GROWTH,
WHICH WOULD BLOCK LIFE-GIVING
SUNLIGHT FROM ITS HOST.
HOWEVER, WATER IS QUICKLY
CHANNELLED AWAY VIA THE 'DRIP
TIPS' OF THE LEAVES SHOWN HERE,
WHICH ARE CHARACTERISTIC OF
RAINFOREST PLANTS: ALSO
COMMON IS A WAXY, SHINY LEAF
SURFACE, WHICH AIDS WATER
RUNOFF AND MAKES THE LEAF
TOUGHER FOR PREDATORS TO EAT.

71

72

**72 THORNS ON SAPLING, MARACÁ**
(William Milliken/Royal Geographic Society
Maracá Rainforest Project)
THE DEFENCES EVOLVED BY
PLANTS AGAINST THEIR PREDATORS
MAY BE STRUCTURAL AS WELL AS
CHEMICAL, AND THOUGH
CLUMSIER MAY BE JUST AS
EFFECTIVE AS LEAF COMPOUNDS.
THE THORNS ON THE TRUNK OF
THIS SAPLING ARE AN EFFECTIVE
DETERRENT. IN SOME TREE
SPECIES, THORNS ARE PRESENT ON
THE SAPLING BUT ARE SHED WHEN
THE MATURE TREE DEVELOPS
DEFENSIVE CHEMICAL COMPOUNDS.

73

**73 RESIN OF PTEROCARPUS SOYAUXII, CAMEROON** (Mike Harrison/Dja River Films)
ALL TREES HAVE RESINOUS SAP WHICH QUICKLY RISES TO SEAL ANY WOUNDS OR
ABRASIONS IN THE BARK OR WOOD. THIS IS IMPORTANT IN PREVENTING EITHER
AN INFECTION ENTERING THE PLANT, OR INSECTS TRYING TO COLONIZE THE
UNPROTECTED WOOD BENEATH THE BARK. THE STINGLESS BEES SHOWN HERE
ARE GATHERING THE OOZING RESIN FOR USE IN THE DEFENCE OF THEIR OWN
NEST ENTRANCE.

# CHAPTER FOUR

# THE UNWITTING MATCHMAKERS:
# FERTILIZATION BY MANIPULATION
## PROFESSOR GHILLEAN T. PRANCE

*Once the plant has successfully defended itself against predators, its second imperative must be to reproduce. For the flowering trees, shrubs and herbs, fertilization must first take place: pollen grains from male flower parts need to be transferred to the female flower parts. But plants cannot move and so must find other means of transporting their pollen. Many employ animals, birds, bats and insects in particular, as carriers. But how can a simple plant manipulate such creatures into helping it to reproduce? The secret lies in its flowers: each one is an alluring target whose colour, scent and structure is designed to attract a specific, though unwitting, pollinator.*

MOST FLOWERING PLANT SPECIES MUST BE POLLI-nated in order to produce seed. The dust-like pollen grains of the flower are its sperm which must be carried to the ovule of another flower in order to fertilize it. In temperate oak and pine forests this process is relatively straightforward; but in tropical rainforests where individual trees of any species are scattered throughout the forest in order to protect themselves from predators and fungal diseases, the process is more complicated. Wind pollination, so successful in temperate regions, here will not work, not only because of the distances involved but also because of the dense canopy under which the air hangs motionless. Rainforest plants therefore rely on animals and in-

---

74 EUGLOSSINE BEE LEAVING ORCHID WITH POLLEN, COSTA RICA
(David Thompson/OSF)
THE INTERDEPENDENCE OF RAINFOREST SPECIES IS EPITOMIZED BY THE
RELATIONSHIP BETWEEN SEVERAL TYPES OF ORCHID AND THEIR POLLINATORS.
CLEARLY, MANY ANIMALS DEPEND ON PLANTS FOR FOOD; EQUALLY, MANY
PLANTS DEPEND ON ANIMALS, IN SOME CASES A SINGLE SPECIES, IN ORDER TO
REPRODUCE. THIS ORCHID NEEDS THE ATTENTION OF THE MALE OF THIS BEE
SPECIES TO FERTILIZE IT BY CARRYING ITS POLLEN TO ANOTHER FLOWER: ITS
ENTIRE STRUCTURE IS GEARED TOWARDS TRAPPING THE BEE, REMOVING POLLEN
IT IS ALREADY CARRYING AND STICKING ITS OWN POLLEN ONTO THE BEE'S BODY.
IN RETURN, IT PROVIDES THE BEE WITH AN ARRAY OF EXOTIC PERFUMES WHICH
THE BEE WILL USE IN TURN TO ATTRACT FEMALES. LIKE MANY OTHER
RAINFOREST PLANTS AND ANIMALS, NEITHER ORCHID NOR BEE COULD SURVIVE
WITHOUT THE OTHER, A GRAPHIC EXAMPLE OF THE COMPLEXITY AND FRAGILITY
OF THE RAINFOREST ECOSYSTEM.

sects for their pollination. Somehow they must attract pollinators, often over distances as great as several hundred metres, and in response to this need a number of extremely precise methods of pollination have evolved.

Typical pollinators are strong fliers that forage over long distances: birds, bats, hawk moths and large bees are the most common. However, strong flight alone is not sufficient. Such precision is needed that pollinators and the plants that they pollinate often evolve in partnership. The petal tube of many hummingbird-pollinated flowers has gradually evolved over thousands of generations so that it corresponds exactly in length and curvature to the beak of the bird, just as the tube of moth-pollinated flowers is precisely the same length as the moth's tongue.

Trees have evolved different flowering strategies to match the lifestyle of their pollinators. Some adopt the 'big bang' approach, such as *Tabebuia*, dropping all their leaves and then producing a mass of yellow or purple flowers in a single dramatic show which attracts the swarms of small bees on which they rely for pollination. Others with larger pollinators such as bats or birds pursue the 'steady state' strategy producing very few flowers per cluster, or even just one, each day. The pollinator's hunger is not satisfied by the nectar of a single tree, and so it must search for another tree to survive. Bat-pollinated plants have adapted to the needs of their nocturnal pollinators, which navigate by sonar, by providing white or lightly coloured flowers which open at night and are easily accessible. They also contain large quantities of nectar to satisfy the substantial appetites of these large, active creatures. Among the many bat-pollinated rainforest plants, the pantropical genus parkia is one of the most spectacular, and its relationship with bats is known in detail owing to the work of Dr Helen Hopkins, who spent many hours on climbing ropes in the rainforest canopy watching how they operate. Parkias produce flower clusters that resemble pom-poms, which in some species hang down on long stalks below the canopy of the tree (a common feature in bat-pollinated trees as bats cannot easily fly in the leafy canopy without damaging their wings) and in others emerge well above the crown. Each cluster has a mass of pollen-bearing stamens all over its surface, so that when a bat alights for an instant to sip the abundant nectar from the top or base of the pom-pom its fur is liberally dusted with pollen, which it transports inadvertently to the next cluster. As the clusters on any one tree mature at different times the bats must fly from tree to tree to find sufficient food, effecting cross-pollination.

In the rainforests of the Americas a group of bats called Microchiroptera are adapted to nectar feeding, while in the Old World a different, distantly related, order, the Megachiroptera, are the flower visitors. However, so well adapted are they to the needs of bats that if bat-pollinated plants are transplanted from one continent to another, as for instance when the South American calabash is grown in Indonesia, they are usually recognized and visited by the local bats.

Not all night-blooming flowers are pollinated by bats. Moth-pollinated plants produce white flowers, strongly and sweetly perfumed, with their nectar hidden in long tubes or spurs. *Tanaecium nocturnum* is a vine used by the Paumari indians as a hallucinogenic snuff. Only the hawk-moth is capable of pollinating it, for alone amongst the nocturnal creatures it does not need to land on the delicate tubular flowers, but can hover near them and pry into them with its long tongue, reaching down to the nectar at the bottom of the 17 centimetre (6½ inch) tube.

Although many rainforest plants are visited by nocturnal creatures, most open their blooms by day and are pollinated principally by bees, butterflies and birds. Rainforest bees fulfil the necessary requirements for pollinators, being large, strong fliers that forage over long distances. Ecologist Daniel Janzen found that euglossine or orchid bees returned to their nest when released from a distance of twenty-three kilometres (fourteen miles). As large orchid bees, together with carpenter bees and bumble bees, have regular daily routes which they follow faithfully from one flowering tree to another, they are the pollinators of many rainforest species.

The brazil nut tree produces large yellow flowers capped by a coiled hood that covers the other flower parts and protects them from predators. To gain access to the nectar inside the hood, the bee must lift it, a feat that only large bees – mostly female orchid bees – are strong enough to accomplish. As they lift the hood their backs press against the pollen-bearing stamens, which dust them with the pollen which they then carry from flower to flower. The tauari tree, a Brazil nut relative, has an even more complex, double coiled hood, from which only a long-tongued orchid bee can extract the nectar, for its tongue is the exact length of the coiled passageway.

Male orchid bees are solitary wanderers who have evolved a relationship with orchids, visiting the flowers to collect fragrances which they pack into cavities on their swollen hind legs. As they do so they inadvertently pick up the pollen-mass of the orchid which, firmly stuck to the bee, is transported from flower to flower. Once they have gathered enough perfume the brightly coloured bees form a swarm that performs a series of complicated flight and buzz rituals to attract the female bees for mating. The brazil nut trees are therefore dependent for their pollination not only on the orchid bees but also on the presence in the forest of the correct species of orchid to provide scent for the male bees so the species can reproduce.

Of all rainforest plants on the three tropical continents figs are amongst the most common, from the cathedral-like banyan with its many trunks and aerial roots to the strangling figs which embrace and eventually smother their host tree. Their pollination system is the most closely co-evolved of all rainforest species. Figs and their wasp pollinators are so closely linked that every species of fig has its own species of wasp that spends most of its life inside the fig. The two organisms are completely interdependent.

The young fig is actually a closed flower cluster containing three types of flower: female flowers that produce the seed, a smaller number of male flowers that produce the pollen and gall flowers, which are specially adapted to hold the wasp's eggs and larvae. When the female flowers mature, several weeks before the male ones, the pollen-loaded wasps enter the fig via a special hidden entrance: the female wasps lay their eggs in the special gall flowers and then die. When the male flowers mature, fifteen to a hundred days later depending on the species, the next generation of wasps emerges from the gall flowers in perfect synchrony. The wingless male wasps mate with the females, then bore a hole through the wall of the fig for their female siblings to emerge. Their function fulfilled, the males then die. The female wasps meanwhile search for pollen in the male flowers, load it into special pollen-carrying structures on their bodies and fly on to another female-phase fig to deposit their pollen and begin the cycle all over again. She has to fly to a different tree because figs are synchronized to be in one phase at any time: pollination is thus relatively guaranteed.

Other rainforest plants depend on a great variety of different animals to carry their pollen and manipulate them in wonderful ways: there are the scarab beetles that are trapped for a day inside the flowers of certain anona flowers before being released again covered with pollen, the many butterflies that visit the slender, delicate forest flowers and those such as the brush-like terminalia or the rice rats that sip nectar from Blakea flowers in the cloud forests of Costa Rica. But the few here described illustrate how the diversity of rainforest trees depends on an equal diversity of animals. Pollination is not a chance event in the rainforest. It is a precise delivery of a tiny dust-like grain to another flower of the same species over a distance of hundreds of metres. This is only possible because of the way in which plants and animals have evolved together in a mutually dependent lift style that affects their structure, their chemistry and the timing of many events in their life cycle.

---

75  **WILD GINGER IN FLOWER, MALAYSIA** (Ken Preston-Mafham/Premaphotos)
THE NECTAR-FILLED BRACTS OF THIS GINGER ATTRACT ANTS, WHICH PROBABLY PROTECT THE PLANT FROM BEING EATEN BUT DO NOT POLLINATE IT. HIDDEN FROM THE LARGER FLYING ANIMALS BECAUSE IT GROWS ON THE DARK FOREST FLOOR, THE GINGER FLOWER IS PROBABLY POLLINATED BY FLIES.

76

*76* **TREES FLOWERING IN THE
CANOPY, SOUTH AMERICA**
(Tony Morrison/South American Pictures)

*77* **FLOWERING IN THE CANOPY,
ATLANTIC RAINFOREST, BRAZIL**
(Luiz Claudio Marigo)
IN RAINFORESTS, UNLIKE IN
TEMPERATE FORESTS, TREES OF
THE SAME SPECIES TEND TO BE
WIDELY SPACED. THIS PRESENTS A
PROBLEM FOR THE PLANT, WHOSE
POLLINATORS MUST FLY DIRECTLY
FROM ONE TREE TO ANOTHER OF
THE SAME SPECIES EVEN THOUGH
ANOTHER ONE MAY BE FAR AWAY.
MANY SPECIES OF CANOPY TREE, IN
WHAT IS CALLED THE 'BIG BANG'
STRATEGY, FLOWER ALL AT ONCE
OVER A WIDE AREA: THEIR
COLOURFUL FLOWERS CONTRAST
WITH THE GREEN BACKGROUND
AND ATTRACT A MASS OF INSECTS.
AS THERE ARE COMPARATIVELY
FEW OTHER TREES IN FLOWER AT
THE SAME TIME, THE TREE
THEREBY ENSURES THAT INSECTS
WILL FLY DIRECTLY FROM ONE TO
ANOTHER OF ITS KIND, ENSURING
POLLINATION.

78

**78 PURPLE PASSION FLOWER VINE, COSTA RICA**

(Michael and Patricia Fogden)
LIKE MANY FLOWERS IN BOTH TROPICAL AND TEMPERATE CLIMATES, PASSION FLOWERS EXUDE SUGARY LIQUID NECTAR, A TEMPTING FOOD WHICH IS RICH IN ENERGY AND IS BAIT FOR A WIDE VARIETY OF POLLINATORS. AS THE ANIMAL DRINKS THE NECTAR, IT INADVERTENTLY COLLECTS POLLEN FROM THE FLOWER.

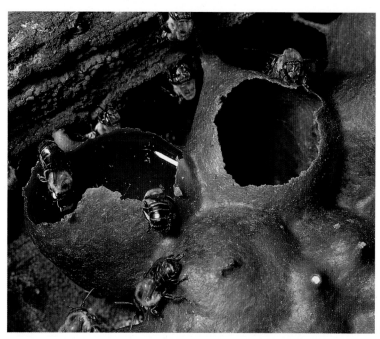

79

**79 STINGLESS BEES AT NEST WITH 'HONEYPOTS', PANAMA**

(Sean Morris/OSF)
MOST PLANTS MUST OFFER SOME REWARD TO THEIR PROSPECTIVE POLLINATORS IN ORDER TO ATTRACT THEM. ENERGY-RICH NECTAR IS ONE OF THE MOST COMMON BAITS, BUT THESE STINGLESS BEES, ONE OF MANY SPECIES IN THE AMERICAN AND AFRICAN RAINFORESTS, ALSO ACTIVELY SEEK THE POLLEN ITSELF. FROM NECTAR THE BEES MAKE HONEY TO BE STORED IN THE 'HONEYPOTS' SHOWN, WHICH ARE MOULDED FROM AN AMALGAM CONTAINING COLLECTED TREE RESIN; WHILE POLLEN FEEDS THE YOUNG BROOD, THE FUTURE COLONY OF BEES.

**80  RAFFLESIA, SUMATRA** (Andrew Mitchell)
THE RAFFLESIA GROWS IN SOUTH-EAST ASIA: IT IS THE LARGEST FLOWER IN THE
WORLD AND CAN MEASURE 91CM/3FT ACROSS. IT PARASITIZES THE ROOTS OF
LIANAS: THE FLOWER IS THE ONLY PART OF THE PLANT WHICH EMERGES ABOVE
GROUND. RAFFLESIA ATTRACTS ITS POLLINATORS BY SMELL, BUT UNLIKE THE
SWEETLY SCENTED BEE- AND BUTTERFLY-POLLINATED FLOWERS, THIS FLOWER,
WHICH IS FLY-POLLINATED, SMELLS OF ROTTING MEAT. ITS LURID COLOURS ALSO
IMITATE THOSE OF A CARCASS LYING ON THE FOREST FLOOR.

**81  PASSION FLOWER AND FRUIT, COSTA RICA** (Michael and Patricia Fogden)
BIRD-POLLINATED FLOWERS TEND TO BE LARGE IN SIZE AND COLOURED RED, AS
BIRDS SEEM TO BE SENSITIVE TO THIS END OF THE SPECTRUM AND ATTRACTED
TO BRIGHT COLOURS; SUCH FLOWERS ALSO TEND NOT TO BE HIGHLY SCENTED,
AS SIGHT IS MORE IMPORTANT TO BIRDS THAN SMELL. IN THE AMAZON
HUMMINGBIRDS ARE THE MAIN BIRD POLLINATORS, THEIR ECOLOGICAL
EQUIVALENT THE SUNBIRD POLLINATES THE FLOWERS OF THE AFRICAN AND
ASIAN FORESTS, WHILE IN THE INDO-AUSTRALIAN AREAS THE NECTAR-EATERS
FULFILL THE SAME FUNCTION.

82

83

**82 FLOWER OF CALABASH TREE, TRINIDAD**

(Ken Preston-Mafham/Premaphotos)
THIS TREE, WHOSE CALABASH FRUITS ARE WIDELY USED AS DRINKING AND STORAGE VESSELS IN THE TROPICS, IS BAT-POLLINATED. THE FLOWERS ARE PERFECTLY ADAPTED TO THESE ANIMALS: THEY ARE PALE COLOURED, BRIMFUL OF NECTAR, AND THOUGH SCENTLESS BY DAY, AT NIGHT THEY EXUDE A STRONG SMELL OF SWEATY CHEESE WHICH IS EXTREMELY ATTRACTIVE TO BATS. THEIR STRATEGY IS EVIDENTLY SUCCESSFUL: IT IS NOT UNUSUAL FOR EVERY FLOWER ON THE TREE TO BE POLLINATED AND DEVELOP INTO A FRUIT – NOTE THE YOUNG CALABASHES BEGINNING TO FORM BY THE BASE OF THE FLOWER.

**83 PARKIA BLOSSOM, CAMEROON**

(Phil Agland)
SOME BAT-POLLINATED FLOWERS, SUCH AS THIS PARKIA, MAKE THEMSELVES ACCESSIBLE BY GROWING ON LONG STALKS BELOW THE TREE CANOPY, WHERE THEIR POLLINATORS' DELICATE WINGS ARE LESS EASILY DAMAGED. THE 'SHAVING-BRUSH' STRUCTURE IS TYPICAL OF FLOWERS VISITED BY BATS, EXPOSING POLLEN-COVERED STAMENS WHICH RUB AGAINST THE ANIMAL'S BREAST AS IT ALIGHTS TO SIP THE PARKIA'S ABUNDANT NECTAR.

84

**84 ORCHID, PERU**

(Gunter Ziesler/Bruce Coleman Ltd)

**85 ORCHID, COSTA RICA**

(Peter Ward/Bruce Coleman Ltd)

**86 ORCHID, AUSTRALIA**

(Leo Meier/Weldon Trannies)

**87 ORCHID, BRAZIL**

(Brian Rogers/Biofotos)

85

86

87

**88  ORCHID, SOUTH AMERICA,**
(James Carmichael/NHPA)
RAINFOREST ORCHIDS ARE IN
MANY CASES DEPENDENT ON A
SINGLE POLLINATOR FOR THE
CONTINUATION OF THEIR SPECIES,
AS SHOWN ON PAGE 82. COLOUR
AND SCENT ATTRACT THE BEE, BUT
IT IS THE SHAPE AND FORM OF THE
FLOWER WHICH ENSURE
FERTILIZATION. MANY ORCHIDS
ARE EXTRAORDINARILY COMPLEX
STRUCTURES, WITH FLAPS, GATES,
HOODS AND INTERNAL HOOKS AND
SPIKES, DESIGNED TO COLLECT
POLLEN FROM OTHER FLOWERS
BORNE BY VISITING INSECTS AND
TO TRANSFER ITS OWN POLLEN
ONTO THE BODY OF THE BEE
BEFORE IT DEPARTS.

88

89

89   GREEN HERMIT HUMMINGBIRD, SOUTH AMERICA
(Konrad Wothe/Bruce Coleman Ltd)

90   HUMMINGBIRD AT PASSION FLOWER (Michael and Patricia Fogden)

91   LONG-TAILED HERMIT AT HELICONIA FLOWER, COSTA RICA
(Michael Fogden/Bruce Coleman Ltd)

HUMMINGBIRDS ARE NOT PRINCIPALLY RAINFOREST BIRDS, THOUGH OF THE 235
SPECIES IN SOUTH AMERICA A FAIR NUMBER LIVE IN TROPICAL FORESTS. FEEDING
ON THE CONCENTRATED NECTAR WHICH FUELS THEIR HIGH METABOLISM AND
CEASELESS HOVERING AND DARTING, MANY ARE HIGHLY SPECIALIZED
POLLINATORS. THEIR LONG BILLS ARE OFTEN EXACTLY MATCHED IN LENGTH TO
THE FLOWERS ON WHICH THEY FEED, IN A REMARKABLE EXAMPLE OF
CO-EVOLUTION WHICH ENSURES THAT ONLY A POLLINATOR CAN REACH THE
NECTAR.

90

91

**92 GEOFFROY'S LONG-NOSED BAT, SOUTH AMERICA**
(Stephen Dalton/NHPA)
MANY RAINFOREST BATS ARE POLLINATORS, WITH MANY FOREST TREES RELYING ON THEM FOR THEIR REPRODUCTION. BATS NAVIGATE AND LOCATE FLOWERS BY SONAR AND CAN VISIT NUMEROUS PLANTS IN ONE NIGHT, PAUSING ONLY A FEW SECONDS AT EACH FLOWER. THE POLLEN IS GENERALLY RUBBED ON TO THE BAT'S FUR AS IT CLINGS MOMENTARILY TO THE FLOWER TO LAP THE NECTAR, BUT SOME BATS, LIKE THIS ONE, HOVER, HUMMINGBIRD-LIKE, OVER THE FLOWER TO SUCK NECTAR WITH THEIR LONG TONGUES.

93

94

**93  EULAEMA ORCHID BEE VISITING ORCHID, PERU**
(Michael Fogden/OSF)
MALE ORCHID BEES, AS PART OF THEIR COURTSHIP BEHAVIOUR, GATHER PERFUMES FROM THE ORCHIDS WHICH THEY INADVERTENTLY POLLINATE IN DOING SO. A NUMBER OF THE MALES WILL THEN GATHER TO FORM A SWARM, AND PERFORM A COMPLICATED AND SCENTED DISPLAY WITH THE AIM OF ATTRACTING FEMALES. THE FEMALES, MEANWHILE, ARE ONE OF THE KEY POLLINATORS OF THE BRAZIL-NUT TREE, WHICH PROVIDES ONE OF THE MOST POPULAR OF FOREST PRODUCTS. SPECIES RELATIONSHIPS ARE THUS EXTRAORDINARILY INTERWOVEN IN THE RAINFOREST: IT CAN BE SAID THAT BECAUSE THE MALE BEE RELIES ON ORCHID SCENT TO ATTRACT A MATE – AND SO TO REPRODUCE – THE BRAZIL NUT TREE IS ALSO DEPENDENT ON ORCHIDS.

**94  PARASITIZING WASP LAYING EGGS IN FIG, SOUTH AMERICA**
(Michael and Patricia Fogden)
THE STORY OF FIGS AND THEIR POLLINATORS IS ONE OF THE MOST COMPLEX IN THE RAINFOREST. THERE ARE MANY DIFFERENT SPECIES OF FIG IN THE WORLD'S RAINFORESTS, EACH WITH ITS OWN POLLINATING WASP. FIG AND WASP ARE COMPLETELY DEPENDENT ON EACH OTHER TO SURVIVE; A PARASITIC, NON-POLLINATING WASP HERE LAYING HER EGGS IN THE WASP LARVAE INSIDE THE FIG IS EQUALLY DEPENDENT ON BOTH FIG AND WASP. BUT THE RELATIONSHIP BETWEEN FIGS AND WASPS HAS A WIDER IMPLICATION. THE FIG IS ONE OF THE MAJOR FRUITING TREES IN THE FOREST, PROVIDING FOOD FOR A WIDE RANGE OF ANIMALS; SO, BY EXTENSION, FIG WASPS CAN BE SAID TO SUPPORT A MAJOR PART OF THE FOREST ECOSYSTEM.

**95   DIRCENNA DERO BUTTERFLY
AT FLOWER, PERU**

(Ken Preston-Mafham/Premaphotos)

THE FLOWERS OF THIS DELICATE
VINE ARE TYPICALLY FORMED TO
ATTRACT BUTTERFLIES. THEY ARE
COLOURED WHITE SO THAT THEY
SHOW UP IN THE DARK
UNDERSTOREY WHERE THEY
GROW, AND THE NECTAR – AND
REPRODUCTIVE ORGANS – IS
LOCATED DEEP WITHIN THEM. THE
TUBULAR FLOWER IS TOO SMALL
FOR MOST INSECTS TO ENTER BUT
IS ACCESSIBLE TO THE BUTTERFLY'S
LONG AND MOBILE TONGUE.

95

**96  'TIGER' BUTTERFLY ON ASCLEPIAS FLOWER, TRINIDAD**
(Ken Preston-Mafham/Premaphotos)
THOUGH THIS FLOWER IS FREQUENTLY VISITED BY BUTTERFLIES WHICH FEED ON
THE NECTAR, ITS PRIMARY POLLINATORS ARE WASPS. IN AN ATTEMPT TO GET
SOMETHING FOR NOTHING, A SPECIES OF ORCHID IMITATES THE ASCLEPIAS,
GROWING AMONG IT AND TAKING ADVANTAGE OF ITS POLLINATORS – THOUGH
UNLIKE THE REAL FLOWER IT OFFERS NO NECTAR AS A RETURN FOR THEIR
ATTENTIONS.

**97  *LANTANA CAMARA* FLOWER, PERU** (Ken Preston-Mafham/Premaphotos)
WHEREVER IT GROWS THIS FLOWER IS CONSTANTLY ATTENDED BY BUTTERFLIES.
IT IS IDEALLY SHAPED FOR BUTTERFLY FEEDING, PRODUCES COPIOUS NECTAR,
AND GROWS PROFUSELY THROUGHOUT THE TROPICS. ALTHOUGH ITS NATIVE
HOME IS IN SOUTH AMERICA, IT HAS NOW COLONIZED ALL THE CONTINENTS
FROM AFRICA TO ASIA AND AUSTRALIA WHERE, PARTLY AS A RESULT OF THE
BUTTERFLIES' ASSIDUITY IN POLLINATING IT, THE FLOWER HAS BECOME A WEED
AND A PEST.

# CHAPTER FIVE

# SPREADING THE SEEDS – SOWING THE FUTURE FOREST

## Dr Caroline Pannell

*A flower which has been successfully fertilized will, in time, develop into a fruit, containing the seeds of future generations, which must, somehow, be scattered to all the corners of the forest. Typically, rainforest plants exploit the needs of animals for their own ends: they have developed fruits which are sweet and juicy, scented and brightly coloured, sought after by a huge variety of creatures which will eat the flesh and spread the seeds within. The penalty for producing such tempting prizes is that they are eaten as readily by seed destroyers as seed dispersers.*

IT IS VITAL FOR THE FOREST'S SURVIVAL THAT THE numerous seeds produced by an adult plant be carried away both from their parent and from each other, otherwise the young seedlings will be crowded together and have insufficient space and light to grow and develop. They will also be vulnerable to attack by fungi or insect larvae and other animals which feed on the leaves, stems or young shoots, for in such conditions, destructive organisms pass directly from the parent tree to its seedlings and from one seedling to the next. This is moreover the only phase in its life cycle when a plant can be moved to new places, and if offspring from different individuals in the population can be brought near to each other then the pollination and fertilization between distant relations which will eventually follow will be likely to produce more vigorous and successful offspring.

Most rainforest plants are dispersed by animals, including ants, fish, reptiles, birds, bats and non-flying mammals such as

---

98 **PALM FRUITS AND FLOWERS, AMAZON, PERU** (Michael and Patricia Fogden)
AS IN SO MANY ASPECTS OF THE RAINFOREST ECOSYSTEM, THE SECOND STAGE OF
PLANT REPRODUCTION, DISPERSAL, INVOLVES BOTH PLANTS AND ANIMALS IN
CLOSELY INTERTWINED RELATIONSHIPS. PLANTS NEED ANIMALS NOT JUST IN
ORDER TO REPRODUCE, BUT ALSO TO TRANSPORT THEIR OFFSPRING TO OTHER
AREAS. SEEDLINGS WHICH GROW NEAR THE PARENT PLANT ARE VULNERABLE FOR
A NUMBER OF REASONS, SO DISPERSAL IS IMPERATIVE; BUT FIRST, THE ANIMAL
MUST BE TEMPTED.

primates, deer, pigs, bears, civets, rodents, tigers and elephants. Each plant species has its own ecological requirements and complex life cycle, often involving several different animals, each of which may itself be the pollinator or disperser of numerous other plant species, and use yet others as food sources or resting places. When the interactions between all these species are taken into account an extremely complex web of relationships between plants and animals emerges.

In mahogany trees of the genus aglaia, for instance, the fruits of different species may be a source of food for primates and birds as well as bats and other mammals. This large genus of more than a hundred species is common in the tropical rainforests of the far east, from India to islands in the Pacific and from southern China to Australia; it is especially common in Thailand, the Malay Peninsula, Sumatra, Borneo and New Guinea. In all these places, except New Guinea (where primates do not occur), some species of aglaia are dispersed by monkeys, gibbons or, in Sumatra and Borneo, by orang utans.

The fruits of these species hang down from the branches in large bunches and so are easily accessible to primates, which break open the protective inedible fruit wall with their hands and mouths to reach the flesh within. Often, these fruits are coloured orange, which is thought to be particularly attractive to primates, and have flesh which smells good to the human nose and is sweet because it contains sugars and sweet-tasting amino acids. The flesh sticks firmly to the rest of the seed which thus tends to be swallowed along with it; however this reproductive part of the seed is not digested but emerges in the faeces, and can then germinate.

For birds the aglaia story is rather different. The fruits of species dispersed by birds are usually attached to a sturdy branch or twig on which they can perch. The protective outer layer breaks open when the fruit is ripe so that the seeds are exposed and birds can peck them out individually with their beaks. In some species the edible outer layer of the seed contains more oil than is found in almost any other kind of plant tissue. So whereas the primate fruit appeals to the sweet tooth of its dispersers, the bird fruit provides a highly concentrated source of energy in the form of the maximum food for the minimum weight, an important advantage for flying animals. The birds swallow the whole seed, but their guts quickly remove the nutritious oily flesh, which in this case does not adhere firmly to the rest of the seed, and the cleaned seed either passes rapidly through the gut to be expelled in the faeces or is regurgitated. These fruits have layers of contrasting colours: a pink or brick-red outer surface, attractive to birds, opens up to reveal a white inside with the seed and its flesh covered with a red skin. The seeds vary in size: many small birds such as bulbuls, barbets and broadbills can swallow the smaller ones, while only pigeons and hornbills can swallow the largest.

Neither birds nor primates usually expel the seeds from their body until they have moved away from the tree in which they consumed them, which means that they are carried away from their parent tree – perhaps as little as ten metres (though it can be up to a hundred) or, in the case of a hornbill, as much as several kilometres. Exceptionally, a seed may remain inside the body of an animal while it migrates across hundreds of kilometres. The larger the animal (elephants, for instance, are important dispersers in some African forests), the more likely it is to cover long distances.

Many other species bear similar sorts of fruit, but there is also a wide range of fruits which attract animals in different ways. In some low-growing plants a tiny oily excrescence on each seed attracts ants, which are their main dispersers.

Other fruits are fleshy and edible on the outside, but have a fruit wall forming a stony layer around the seed to protect it from being digested. In some large rainforest trees which can exploit the air currents above the canopy, the fruit does not have a fleshy layer at all, but the seed has a wing and is dispersed by wind, and in others the fruit wall is corky so that the fruits can float away on river or ocean currents.

The single most important source of food for the fruit-eating animals of tropical rainforests throughout the world is the fig. Any one area of forest may have twenty different species of fig, ranging from small treelets to enormous strangling or banyan figs which bear many hundreds of kilograms of fruits. Almost any fruit-eating animal that can fly or climb will visit these giant trees to feast on the fruits, while many other animals feed on those which fall to the ground. In Central America twenty-six species of birds in ten families have been observed taking the fruits of only one species, and in west Malaysia thirty-two species of vertebrates have been recorded feeding on a single tree. Fig seeds have even been found in quantity in the stomach of the Amazonian fish *Triportheus elongatus*.

Because of their complex pollination system, the trees of any one fig species do not all bear fruit at the same time, but in succession through the year. If figs were not available in this way the forest would not be able to support its fruit-eating animals in anything like their present abundance and diversity, which in turn would mean far fewer animals would be available for the dispersal of seeds of other plant species.

Fig seeds are so widely dispersed that they can be found nearly everywhere within the range of the genus. This highly efficient dispersal system is reflected in the abundance of figs in the early stages of forest succession and their diversity on some newly formed or remote islands. Within thirty years of its formation, twelve species of fig had colonized a lava flow on Mount Cameroon in West Africa. Figs were among the first trees to appear on Krakatoa, a group of volcanic islands off south-west Java, after their cataclysmic eruption in 1883. Nine species of fig have also been successfully dispersed to the volcanic island of San Tomé in the Gulf of Guinea, more than 300 kilometres (190 miles) from the African mainland. The great majority of woody plants on San Tomé have fleshy fruits which must have been brought there by the fruit-eating birds and bats which have colonized the island. This silvicultural role of dispersers, though more obvious in the case of entirely new habitats such as volcanic islands, is even more important – though less easily studied – in existing rainforest on the mainland.

In addition to these animals which eat only the fleshy parts of the ripe fruit and do not damage the seed there are many which obtain their nourishment from the unripe fruit or the seeds. The seeds of many forest trees are large and nutritious, so as to provide food for the seedling when it germinates. Some dispersers obtain their food not from the fruit wall, but from the seed itself. While they may be responsible for destroying a large proportion of the seed crop, they may also accidentally drop or bury some seeds which they never recover, and which are thus able to germinate. The great majority of animals that eat seeds are not dispersers, however, and to protect against their attacks the seed may contain toxic or bitter chemicals or be sheathed in a stony fruit wall or seed coat. Many seeds are nevertheless destroyed by insect larvae, especially of bruchid beetles and weevils, or by vertebrates such as parrots or squirrels, which overcome the seed's defences either by detoxifying the noxious chemicals or by cracking open or gnawing through the protective layer surrounding the seed.

It is clear from even a very brief consideration of relationships within the rainforest ecosystem that the old assumption that the regeneration of trees is spontaneous and independent of other living organisms must be revised. Trees continue to live for tens or hundreds of years after the animals upon which they depend for reproduction disappear, but if these animals have been lost for ever, then the trees are biologically dead. The full impact of the current destruction of the rainforest may not be realized until well into the twenty-first century, by which time it may be too late to find out which inter-species relationships ensured the continuity of the forest, and more importantly, to put the relevant plants and animals back.

---

**99  GIANT FRUIT BAT, SRI LANKA** (Stephen Dalton/NHPA)
BATS CAN MAKE UP OVER HALF THE MAMMALS PRESENT IN RAINFOREST, AND MANY ARE FRUIT-EATERS. BECAUSE THEY FEED PRIMARILY ON LIQUID, BATS TEND TO TAKE THE FRUIT TO A SAFE PERCH, SUCK OUT THE JUICE AND DISCARD THE SEED. ONLY VERY SMALL SEEDS WILL BE INGESTED AND PASSED OUT IN THE BAT'S DROPPINGS AS IT FLIES OVER THE FOREST. BECAUSE THEY ARE DISPERSERS FOR A NUMBER OF IMPORTANT TREES, A REDUCTION IN THE NUMBER OF BATS CAN RESULT IN THE DISAPPEARANCE OF MANY SPECIES OF TREE. FRUIT BATS IN THE AFRICAN AND INDIAN FORESTS HAVE LONG BEEN HUNTED IN SMALL NUMBERS FOR THEIR HIGH-QUALITY MEAT: WITH THE INCREASING USE OF GUNS, MANY MORE BATS ARE BEING LOST AND SEVERAL SPECIES ARE ON THE BRINK OF EXTINCTION.

**100  SCARLET MACAW, SOUTH AMERICA** (Gerry Ellis/Ellis Wildlife Collection)
ALTHOUGH MANY BIRDS EAT THE FRUITS AND INADVERTENTLY DISPERSE THE
SEEDS THEY CONTAIN, OTHERS ACTUALLY EAT AND DESTROY THE SEEDS. PRIME
AMONG THESE SEED PREDATORS ARE THE PARROTS AND MACAWS, WHICH
REMOVE THE OUTER FLESHY FRUIT COATING WITH THEIR CLAWS AND BEAKS,
THEN CRUNCH THE KERNEL. THE MOUTHPARTS OF THE MACAWS HAVE EVOLVED
TO BE PHENOMENALLY STRONG, AND THEY CAN CRACK EVEN THE HARDEST
SHELLS. MANY SPECIES OF MACAW AND PARROT ARE NOW SERIOUSLY
ENDANGERED, OWING TO THEIR COLLECTION FOR THE WESTERN ANIMAL TRADE

101

**101  RESPLENDENT QUETZAL, CLOUD FOREST, COSTA RICA**
(Michael and Patricia Fogden)
THE RARE AND BEAUTIFUL QUETZAL, SACRED BIRD OF THE ANCIENT MAYANS, IS
NOW ENDANGERED. THE QUETZAL IS DEPENDENT ON THE WILD AVOCADO
WHICH FORMS A HIGH PROPORTION OF ITS DIET; LIKEWISE, THE AVOCADO
DEPENDS ON THE QUETZAL, WHICH IS ITS PRIMARY DISPERSER. PREVIOUSLY,
QUETZALS WERE NOT VULNERABLE, BUT THE LOSS OF THEIR PRIMARY FOOD
SOURCE TO THE LOGGING COMPANIES (AVOCADOS ARE A FAVOURED TIMBER
TREE), AND SOME POACHING TO MAKE STUFFED BIRDS FOR THE TOURIST TRADE,
HAS NOW SERIOUSLY REDUCED THEIR NUMBERS.

102

102   **TOUCAN, BELIZE** (Simon Zisman/Remote Source)

103   **SAFFRON TOUCANET, SOUTH AMERICA** (Luiz Claudio Marigo)

104   **RHINOCEROS HORNBILL, MALAYSIA** (Morten Strange/NHPA)
CENTRAL AND SOUTH AMERICAN TOUCANS AND TOUCANETS AND THEIR OLD
WORLD EQUIVALENTS, THE HORNBILLS, ARE IMPORTANT DISPERSERS OF FRUIT IN
THE FOREST. THESE BIRDS OFTEN EAT FRUIT WITH QUITE LARGE SEEDS, GAINING
NUTRITION FROM THE JUICY SEED COATING AND SWALLOWING THE
UNDAMAGED SEED WHOLE. BECAUSE MOST BIRDS AIM TO GET RID OF HEAVY
AND NUTRITIONALLY USELESS SEEDS AS SOON AS POSSIBLE, THEY OFTEN
REGURGITATE THEM RATHER THAN PASS THEM OUT IN THEIR DROPPINGS, BUT
SUCH LARGE AND POWERFUL FLIERS AS THESE CAN STILL COVER A
CONSIDERABLE DISTANCE BEFORE DOING SO.

103

104

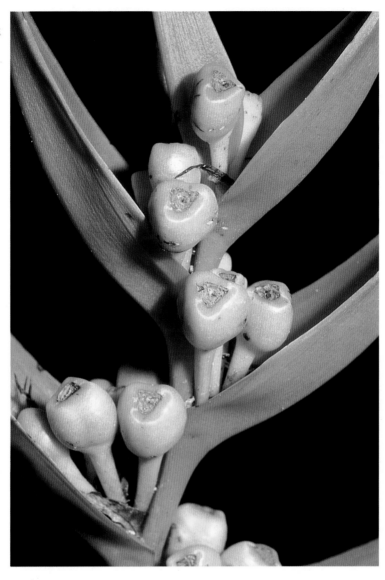

105

**105  HELICONIA FRUIT, VENEZUELA** (Ken Preston-Mafham/Premaphotos)
THE BEAUTIFUL HELICONIA, OR 'LOBSTER-CLAW', FLOWER IS POLLINATED BY
HUMMINGBIRDS AND THEN DEVELOPS SMALL, BERRY-LIKE FRUITS. MOST SPECIES
TEND TO BE DISPERSED BY THE BIRDS WHICH FREQUENT THE UNDERSTOREY
WHERE THESE PLANTS GROW.

**106  PALM FRUIT, SOUTH AMERICA** (Ken Preston-Mafham/Premaphotos)
THE MANY SPECIES OF PALM FRUITS ARE DISPERSED PRIMARILY BY BATS, BIRDS
AND SMALL MAMMALS, WHICH WILL CARRY OFF THOSE WHICH FALL TO THE
GROUND. IN AFRICA, FRUIT BATS ARE NOW REGULARLY BEING SHOT BECAUSE
THEY TAKE VALUABLE FRUITS FROM PLANTATIONS OF THE ECONOMICALLY
IMPORTANT OIL PALM.

**107 DIANELLA FRUITS, BORNEO**
(Ken Preston-Mafham/Premaphotos)

**108 PSYCHOTRIA FRUITS, VENEZUELA**
(Ken Preston-Mafham/Premaphotos)
IT IS NOT KNOWN FOR CERTAIN WHAT DISPERSES THESE FRUITS, BUT THEIR SMALL SIZE (ABOUT THAT OF A HAWTHORN BERRY) SUGGESTS THAT THEY MAY BE EATEN BY BIRDS. AN AFRICAN RELATIVE OF THE PSYCHOTRIA FRUIT IS KNOWN TO BE BIRD-DISPERSED.

107

108

109

**109 COCCOCYPSELUM FRUIT, TRINIDAD** (Ken Preston-Mafham/Premaphotos)

**110 POIKILOSPERMUM FRUIT, SWAMP, MALAYSIA** (Ken Preston-Mafham/Premaphotos)
ALTHOUGH THE ATTRACTIVE PROPERTIES OF CERTAIN COLOURS TO CERTAIN
ANIMALS ARE WELL KNOWN (FOR INSTANCE, RED ATTRACTS BIRDS WHILE
ORANGE DRAWS MONKEYS), THE PURPOSE OF THESE VIVID BLUES AND PURPLES,
UNKNOWN IN TEMPERATE ZONES, IS UNCERTAIN. ONE POSSIBILITY IS THAT BLUE
IS A NOTICEABLE COLOUR WHEN LIT FROM ABOVE IN THE DARKNESS OF THE
FOREST LOWER LAYERS, AND THUS IS ATTRACTIVE TO BIRDS AND RODENTS
WHICH FORAGE ON THE FLOOR. BLUES AND PURPLES ARE ALSO KNOWN TO BE
ATTRACTIVE TO BIRDS OF THE PHEASANT FAMILY, WHILE CROWS AND STARLINGS
ARE DRAWN TO BRIGHT AND SHINY OBJECTS.

110

111

112

113

**111 'LITTLE LEMONS', COSTA RICA**
(Ken Preston-Mafham/Premaphotos)

**112 DYSOXYLUM FRUITS AND FLOWERS, NEW GUINEA**
(Ken Preston-Mafham/Premaphotos)

**113 MEDINILLA FRUITS, BORNEO**
(Ken Preston-Mafham)
SOME TREES PRODUCE FRUITS AND FLOWERS DIRECTLY FROM THEIR TRUNKS. THEIR FLOWERS AND FRUITS TEND TO BE LARGE AND BRIGHTLY COLOURED, NOTICEABLE IN THE DARKNESS OF THE UNDERSTOREY AND, BECAUSE OF THEIR MANNER OF GROWTH, EASILY ACCESSIBLE TO POLLINATING AND SEED DISPERSING ANIMALS. WHILE THEIR CANOPY-FLOWERING RELATIONS USE ONE SET OF ANIMALS, THESE PLANTS TAKE ADVANTAGE OF QUITE A DIFFERENT 'SUITE' OF ANIMALS LIVING BELOW THE CANOPY: ANTS AND OTHER CRAWLING INSECTS, BATS (MANY OF WHICH PREFER THE LOWER, CLEARER AREAS OF THE FOREST), CERTAIN BIRDS WHICH LIVE IN THE LOWER SHRUB LAYERS, AND TERRESTRIAL MONKEYS.

114

**114 HEDYCHIUM FRUITS, BORNEO**
(Ken Preston-Mafham/Premaphotos)

**115 UNIDENTIFIED FRUIT,
VENEZUELA**
(Ken Preston-Mafham/Premaphotos)
THE FRUITS SHOWN HERE HAVE
DEHISCED, THAT IS, SPLIT OPEN TO
REVEAL THE SEED WITHIN. IN BOTH
CASES, THE SEED CONTRASTS WITH
THE REVEALED INTERIOR OF THE
SEED CASE: ORANGE AND PINK IN
ONE CASE, RED AND BLACK IN THE
OTHER. SUCH VIVID COLOURS ARE
ATTRACTIVE TO MONKEYS, BUT
EVEN MORE SO TO BIRDS, WHICH
RELY ALMOST EXCLUSIVELY ON
SIGHT FOR FINDING FOOD AND
SEEM PARTICULARLY DRAWN TO
CONTRASTING COLOURS: RED AND
BLACK IS AN ESPECIALLY COMMON
COMBINATION FOR BIRD-
DISPERSED FRUITS.

115

117

**116  BREADFRUIT, COSTA RICA**
(Ken Preston-Mafham/Premaphotos)

**117  RATTAN FRUITS, AUSTRALIA**
(Ken Preston-Mafham/Premaphotos)
BREADFRUIT (116) IS A STAPLE FOOD
FOR MANY PEOPLE AND IS NOW
PLANTED ALL OVER THE TROPICS,
OBVIATING THE NEED FOR BATS,
ITS NATURAL DISPERSERS. MANY
PEOPLE ALSO RELY ON THE
RATTANS, THE STRONG, PLIABLE
CLIMBING PALMS OF SOUTH EAST
ASIA, WHICH ARE USED TO MAKE
ROPE, FURNITURE ETC. IT IS NOT
KNOWN WHICH OF THE BIRDS,
BATS, SQUIRRELS AND MONKEYS
THAT EAT THE FRUITS DISPERSE
THEM, BUT IN HEALTHY FOREST
THERE ARE ABUNDANT SEEDLINGS.
RATTANS HOWEVER CANNOT
SURVIVE ON DISTURBED LAND SO,
AS THE RAINFORESTS DISAPPEAR,
THEIR EXISTENCE IS THREATENED.

118

**118  BRAZIL NUT, AMAZONIA**
(Steve Bowles)
THIS FRUIT CONTAINS A CLUSTER
OF THE BRAZIL NUTS WHICH ARE
SO FAMILIAR TO US: WHEN RIPE,
THE 'LID' OF THE FRUIT BREAKS
OPEN. THE EXTREMELY HARD
SHELLS OF THE NUTS WITHIN ARE
RESISTANT TO ALL PREDATORS
EXCEPT THE AGOUTI (124);
HOWEVER, ALTHOUGH THE AGOUTI
DESTROYS MANY SEEDS, ITS HABIT
OF BURYING, HOARDING, AND
FORGETTING THE NUTS ALSO
HELPS TO DISPERSE THEM. BRAZIL
NUTS ARE ONE OF THE MOST
IMPORTANT TROPICAL PRODUCTS,
AND ARE WIDELY EXPORTED TO
EUROPE AND THE UNITED STATES.

**119  PUFFBALL HIT BY RAINDROPS
RELEASING SPORES**
(Michael and Patricia Fogden)
UNLIKE THE FLOWERING PLANTS
OF THE RAINFOREST, MOST FUNGI
ARE STRUCTURALLY ADAPTED TO
SCATTER THEIR OWN DUST-LIKE
REPRODUCTIVE SPORES. THIS
PUFFBALL, WHICH IS SOFT WHEN
YOUNG, BECOMES INCREASINGLY
BRITTLE AND DELICATE AS IT
MATURES. EVENTUALLY, EVEN THE
MINUTE IMPACT OF A RAINDROP
CAUSES THE OUTER CASING TO
EXPLODE, RELEASING A CLOUD OF
SPORES SO LIGHT THAT THEY CAN
BE BORNE FAR AWAY ON THE
SLIGHTEST AIR CURRENT TO
COLONIZE NEW GROUND.

119

120

121

**120 ERVATAMIA FRUIT, QUEENSLAND, AUSTRALIA** (Ken Preston-Mafham)
IN AUSTRALIAN FOREST, WHERE THIS FRUIT GROWS, SEEDS ARE DISPERSED BY
THE USUAL BATS AND BIRDS, BUT THERE ARE NONE OF THE PRIMATES FOUND IN
OTHER AREAS. PRIMATES ARE GENERALLY QUITE IMPORTANT DISPERSERS SIMPLY
BECAUSE THEY EAT SO MUCH FRUIT: HERE, THEIR PLACE IN THE ECOSYSTEM IS
PROBABLY FILLED BY FRUIT EATING MARSUPIALS, BIRDS AND BATS.


**121 RACEMOSA FIGS, AUSTRALIA** (Ken Preston-Mafham/Premaphotos)
THERE ARE ENORMOUS NUMBERS OF FIG SPECIES, WHICH ARE THE SINGLE MOST
IMPORTANT FOOD FOR FRUIT-EATING ANIMALS IN THE RAINFORESTS: IN ASIA
THEY MAKE UP HALF OF ALL THE FRUITS EATEN BY THE LARGE PRIMATES, AND
UP TO FORTY PER CENT OF THE DIET OF FRUIT-EATING ANIMALS IN AMAZONIA.
THEY ARE PROBABLY DISPERSED BY ALL OR MOST OF THE ANIMALS WHICH EAT
THEM, AND ARE HIGHLY SUCCESSFUL PLANTS: BUT THE FAVOUR IS RETURNED,
FOR WITHOUT THE FIGS, THE FOREST WOULD BE UNABLE TO SUPPORT THE HUGE
VARIETY OF FRUIT-EATING BIRDS, MONKEYS, BATS, AND OTHER MAMMALS WHICH
SO ENRICH ITS LIFE.

122

123

124

124

**122  SQUIRREL MONKEY, SOUTH AMERICA** (Konrad Wothe/Bruce Coleman Ltd)

**123  GEOFFROY'S SPIDER MONKEY, COSTA RICA** (Konrad Wothe/Bruce Coleman Ltd)
FRUIT MAKES UP EIGHTY PER CENT OF THE DIET OF BOTH THESE MONKEYS.
MONKEYS PREFER LARGE, BRIGHTLY COLOURED AND SCENTED FRUITS, WHICH
THEY OFTEN EXAMINE FOR RIPENESS BEFORE TASTING. THEY ARE NOT
PARTICULARLY EFFICIENT SEED DISPERSERS, AS THEY TEND TO TAKE ONE OR
TWO BITES FROM A FRUIT AND THEN DROP IT AT THE BASE OF THE TREE;
HOWEVER, SOMETIMES THEY WILL MOVE AWAY TO EAT, AND SOME MONKEY
SPECIES HAVE CHEEK POUCHES IN WHICH THEY STORE FRUIT. ONLY VERY SMALL
SEEDS WILL BE CONSUMED WITH THE FRUIT AND PASSED OUT IN THE
DROPPINGS.

**124  AGOUTI, BRAZIL** (Nick Gordon)
THE AGOUTI IS A LARGE RODENT WITH A VORACIOUS APPETITE FOR SEEDS AND
SEEDLINGS, AND IS ATTRACTED BY THE SOUND OF FALLING FRUITS. ALTHOUGH IT
DESTROYS EVERY SEED IT EATS, IN TIMES OF ABUNDANCE THE AGOUTI BURIES A
STORE OF SEEDS FOR USE WHEN THERE IS LESS FOOD TO BE FOUND.
FREQUENTLY IT FORGETS ITS HOARDS AND THUS HELPS THE DISPERSAL OF MANY
KINDS OF SEEDS.

*CHAPTER SIX*

# BIGGER, BRIGHTER, LOUDER – SIGNALS THROUGH THE LEAVES

### JONATHAN KINGDON

*Rainforest plants, as we have seen, use endless devices to make themselves noticeable and attractive to the animals on which they depend. But animals too must signal, advertise and attract in order to claim territory, court a mate, or warn of approaching danger – and must avoid being eaten in the process. Densely leaved and crowded with an enormous array of different animal species, all of which need to communicate, tropical rainforest presents a challenge to any creature which needs to be noticed. But its very restrictions have led to the evolution of an extraordinary range of spectacular behavioural and physical strategies, designed to attract members of the same species, and avoid those of others.*

TROPICAL RAINFOREST IS NATURE AT ITS MOST crowded and confusing. Tree trunks and foliage obstruct vision and attenuate sound; continuous rain washes scents away; signals of all sorts – visual, olfactory and vocal – have to compete with a cacophony of others. Nevertheless, for most of the inhabitants of the forest there are times when it is imperative to advertize their presence. The only way to do this is with unusually ostentatious colours, smells, movements or noises, which will penetrate the wall of green and distinguish the giver of the signal from the thousands of other species with which it shares the forest.

Modification by elaboration and amplification has become the stuff of communication in this environment, creating beings whose forms are often bigger, brighter, stranger and louder than their counterparts beyond the trees. Thus the forest hornbills are bigger and more boldly coloured than their savanna cousins; they also form larger aggregations and advertize their

---

125 **EYELASH VIPER AMONG PALM FRUITS, COSTA RICA** (Michael and Patricia Fogden)
RAINFOREST ANIMALS AND PLANTS LIVE WITH A CONSTANT DILEMMA: THEY
MUST BE NOTICED BY THE MATES, POLLINATORS AND DISPERSERS ON WHICH
THEY DEPEND, BUT NOT BY PREDATORS, UNLESS THEY CAN WARN THEM AGAINST
EATING THEM, AND NOT BY INTENDED PREY. THE YELLOW EYELASH VIPER USES
ITS VIVID COLORATION TO ATTRACT ANIMALS DRAWN TO BRIGHT COLOURS; IT
PERFECTLY CAMOUFLAGES ITSELF IN RIPE FRUITS WHICH ATTRACT A RANGE OF
FRUIT-EATERS INCLUDING PLENTY OF SUITABLE PREY.

presence with wing feathers which have been modified into noisy wind pumps, and beaks which have become megaphone-like sonators, resounding their calls across the canopy.

As in any habitat, genes cannot be passed on and an organism cannot reproduce itself by remaining quiescent or inconspicuous. Even the most cryptic animal (and rainforest fauna is celebrated for its extraordinary disguises and camouflages) or plant must sometimes advertise its sexual condition or status, using distinctive signals that can be sensed chemically, optically or through vibrations, and which can compete with the accumulated 'noise' of innumerable attention-seeking competitors. Signals can be for many purposes – to threaten, to alert others to danger, to establish the whereabouts of offspring or fellow group members, or merely to make social contact – but the most pressing need for signals in the forest, among both animals and plants, arises from the essential business of reproduction.

It is the variety and number of such signals, their structural ingenuity and sheer flamboyance that impresses almost everyone who enters a rainforest. Sights, sounds and smells assail the senses; the litter of countless reproducing things – fallen fruit and pods, withered flowers and moulted plumes – lies underfoot; the air is heavy with the perfume of flowers and fruit, and, were our noses sensitive enough to smell them, with the mating odours of moths, butterflies, bats and forest pigs, and with scents marking innumerable territories.

For animals, particularly the higher ones, the whole reproductive process is dragged out into complex sequences of courtship, with protracted periods of nesting or the nurturing of young, all of which involve the use of signals. For plants, however, the aim of the signal is essentially to attract an animal which in the space of a few minutes will either collect pollen or seeds for dispersal. Plants have evolved ingenious devices to ensure the success of these essential moments, devices which both attract and manipulate the behaviour of the animals on which they depend. Orchids, relatively rare and often growing in rather inaccessible sites, will go to almost any lengths to attract their pollinators: dummy mates, intoxicating nectar, alighting platforms, spring-loaded traps and clamps, and of course, long-lasting, exquisitely coloured optical targets, are all designed to enlist their services.

Within the animal kingdom, where signals are mainly directed at a member of the same species, the manipulation becomes still more ingenious. The devices used are also more complex, partly because the transmitter of signals is also the receiver. Instead of being an autonomous structure, such as a flower or fruit, the signal must be contrived by modifying a part of the body originally meant for quite another function. Lubricants, sweat or excreta become chemically exact scent signals; air sacs, chords or rasping surfaces generate precisely tuned sounds; and limbs, wings, heads and bodies are painted with flashes of colour, becoming flags to be waved at precise moments. Cock birds of paradise, for instance, converge during the mating season to display their flamboyant plumes in localized 'courts', and leaf-green male anolis lizards inflate their colourful throats to grotesque proportions to attract females. Nocturnal fireflies of both sexes meet by flashing bursts of light, differently coded in each species.

All of these animals are threatened by innumerable predators, and so must keep their moments of conspicuousness to a minimum. The firefly switches its light on and off, the lizard's throat collapses as readily as it inflates, while only the expendable male birds of paradise face the risks during the breeding season. Many animals have completely sacrificed the benefits of visual exhibitionism for safety in camouflage, and have developed aural or olfactory signalling techniques instead.

Visual signals, in fact, are usually only part of a suite which also involves sound and scent. African epauletted fruit bats emit very loud musical notes which necessitate strong muscular spasms of the diaphragm and chest. This is expressed visibly as a flexing of the shoulders, and on the prominence this creates a pocket has formed which enfolds a long tuft of pure white hair. The pocket opens and the 'epaulette' fluffs out in a flash of white which is perfectly synchronized with each spasmodic note. The pocket is also glandular, each eversion sending out a puff of scent so that pulses of sound, light and scent are broadcast together.

To our eyes, however, the most obvious signals by far given by any of the millions of rainforest life forms use colour. One of the most common signalling colours in the forest is red, which may be particularly suitable because it can be coded to attract specific pollinators, dispersers or mates by 'reaching' well into the red end of the spectrum, where only the eyes of a limited number of species are sensitive: some butterflies, fruit bats and hummingbirds are thought to have an especially broad spectrum of colour vision. Being the spectral complementary colour to green, red may also commend itself as a contrasting signal. Thus many turacos, lorikeets, woodpeckers and trogons with normally inconspicuous green liveries may display red flashes on their wings, bodies or heads.

The position and context for such sudden flashing of a bright contrasting colour varies from species to species. In squabbling lorikeets it may be an aggressive 'keep off' notice; in turacos it may be a cohesive follow-my-leader sign; while in woodpeckers, the percussion of the hammering beak on a branch is synchronized with movements of the birds' red head, which may help to establish contact between widely dispersed individuals.

Many canopy-living birds have iridescent plumage and take pains to position themselves correctly vis-à-vis the sun and their partners' eyes in order to create the proper effect. Sunbirds, hummingbirds and glossy starlings give brilliant displays of iridescent greens, purples and blues. Below the canopy, however, glossy colours lose their impact: but one bird which lives permanently in the lower, darker levels of the forest has found an extraordinary solution to this problem. The male magnificent bower bird, having established his courting area on the forest floor, systematically defoliates patches of the canopy far above so that carefully choreographed shafts of sunlight will penetrate his bower, illuminating his iridescent magnificence at the vital moment for the benefit of his intended mate.

Such enormous and protracted efforts show the extreme competitiveness involved in finding a mate, and the importance of visual effects in animal communication. Animals which move in to the forest from another habitat must, by implication, quickly rise to the adaptive challenge if they are to survive. Mandrills, relatively recent arrivals from the savanna, have made just such an evolutionary shift. The male mandrill has evolved a range of lurid colours we normally associate with tropical birds or fish – electric blue, scarlet, yellow and purple.

The ground-dwelling savanna animals from which the mandrills evolved probably resembled modern baboons in using ritualized yawning as a vitally important social signal. Predominantly a male signal, yawning advertises their armoury of canine teeth; when accompanied by a toss of the head, it becomes an even more flamboyant gesture which is conspicuous from a distance. In the poor forest light, however, yawning becomes·an over-energetic and ineffective technique for regulating mandrill society. The evolutionary solution has been to paint a permanent fake snarl around the mouth and muzzle of male mandrills. The bones and tissues have been inflated, folded and tricked out in a blue growl above the area where a 'real' snarl would appear: both the site and the anatomical materials used to construct this elaborate signal have shifted in order to make it more prominent and unambiguous. As a male mandrill ages his snarl steadily inflates, until his field of view is seriously impaired by his own swollen muzzle. The sheer extravagance of it demonstrates how vital visual signals can be, especially for forest animals.

In the densely leaved, densely populated world of the forest, the inhabitants must be highly competitive, both with other species, and with members of their own. Extraordinarily specialised, their modifications, elaborations and amplifications are part of the neverending struggle to see and be seen, to reproduce and survive.

---

**126  RED UAKARI, AMAZON** (Rod Williams/Bruce Coleman Ltd)
LITTLE IS KNOWN ABOUT THE SOCIAL BEHAVIOUR OF THESE MONKEYS, BUT THE BRILLIANT CRIMSON FACE WHICH CONTRASTS BOTH WITH ITS SHAGGY RUST-COLOURED COAT AND THE COMPLEMENTARY GREEN COLOURS OF THE FOREST, IS ALMOST CERTAINLY SIGNAL TO OTHERS OF THE SPECIES.

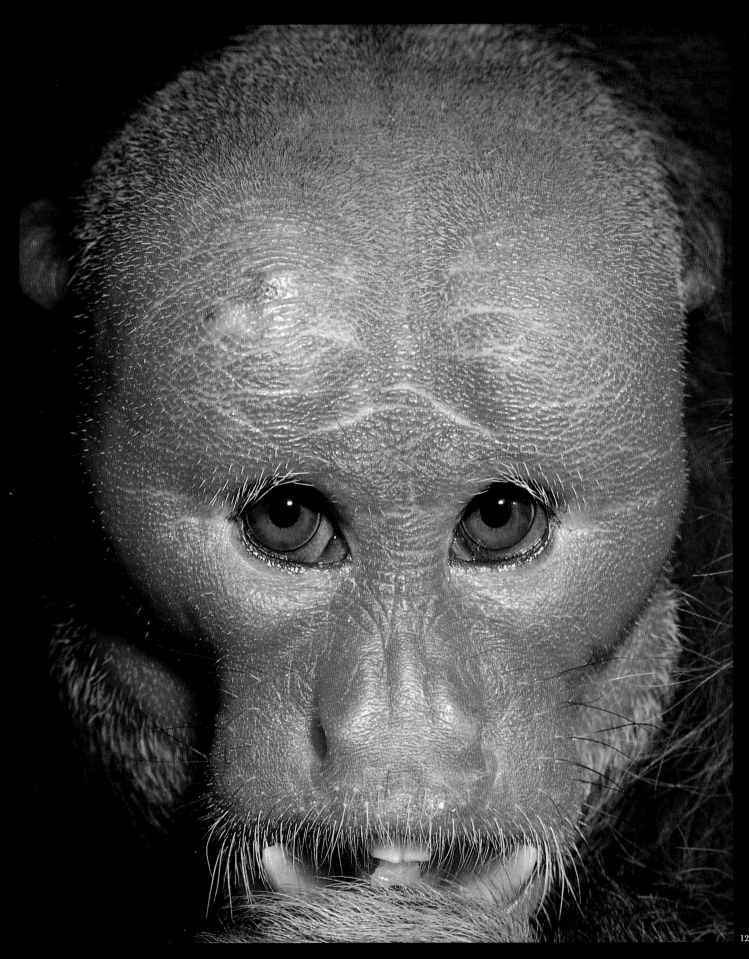

127   **FLAME OF THE FOREST IN BLOSSOM, PUERTO RICO**
(Gerry Ellis/Ellis Wildlife Collection)
AGAINST THE SEA OF GREEN LEAVES WHICH IS THE CANOPY, A FLUSH OF RED BLOSSOMS GIVES A VIBRANT AND IMMEDIATELY OBVIOUS SIGNAL TO THE MANY POTENTIAL POLLINATING INSECTS, PARTICULARLY BEES, WHICH FLY OVER THE FOREST.

127

128

**128 FRUITS OF SHRUB, NEW GUINEA**

(Brian Coates/Bruce Coleman Ltd)
FRUITS NEED TO ATTRACT DISPERSING ANIMALS JUST AS FLOWERS NEED TO FIND POLLINATORS: RED IS A STRONGLY ATTRACTIVE COLOUR FOR BIRDS, PARTICULARLY WHEN CONTRASTED AGAINST THE BLACK OF THE SEED WITHIN.

129

**129 ORCHID, SOUTH AMERICA**

(Michael Fogden/OSF)
AS WELL AS PRESENTING GORGEOUSLY COLOURED OPTICAL TARGETS, ORCHIDS HAVE EVOLVED A WHOLE RANGE OF DEVICES FOR ATTRACTING ANIMALS AND MANIPULATING THEIR BEHAVIOUR. IN A BID TO ENLIST THE HELP OF POLLINATORS, SOME ORCHIDS PRODUCE NECTAR WHICH INTOXICATES BEES, CAUSING THEM TO TUMBLE INSIDE AND UNWITTINGLY POLLINATE THE FLOWER; MANY PROVIDE PERFUMES TO BE COLLECTED BY MALE BEES WHICH IN TURN USE THEM TO ATTRACT A MATE; OTHERS STILL IMITATE FLOWERS WHICH GIVE NECTAR BUT PRODUCE NONE, WHILE IN A SUPREME CONFIDENCE TRICK, SOME EVEN PRODUCE DUMMY MATES.

130

**130 TWO MOTHS, COSTA RICA**
(Michael Fogden/OSF)

**131 TREE FROG, BRAZIL**
(Ken Preston-Mafham/Premaphotos)
DISGUISED AS A DEAD LEAF, ANY
IMMOBILE ANIMAL IS INVISIBLE TO
PREDATORS IN THE FOREST WHERE
LEAVES ARE CONSTANTLY FALLING.
BY DAY, THE TREE FROG HUNCHES,
CRYPTIC, SEVERAL FEET UP IN THE
FOLIAGE, WHERE MANY DEAD
LEAVES ARE TRAPPED; BY NIGHT IT
DESCENDS TO HUNT, AND TO MATE.

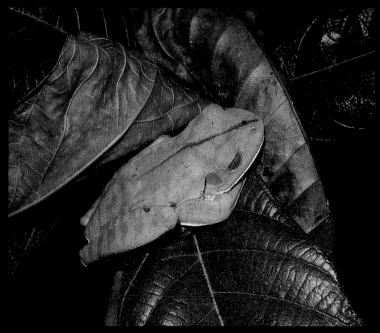

131

132

**132   KATYDID, COSTA RICA**
(Michael and Patricia Fogden)

**133   KATYDID, COSTA RICA**
(Michael and Patricia Fogden)
KATYDIDS CAN BE FOUND IN
TROPICAL FORESTS IN MANY PARTS
OF THE WORLD, WHERE THEY ARE
SUPREME MASTERS OF DISGUISE.
WITH THE OPPORTUNITY FOR
VISUAL SIGNALS TO A MATE
SACRIFICED IN FAVOUR OF
CONCEALMENT, THE SEXES
COMMUNICATE WITH STRIDENT
AURAL SIGNALS, CREATED BY
RUBBING THEIR WINGS TOGETHER,
WHICH ARE INSTANTLY
RECOGNIZABLE TO ANOTHER OF
THE SPECIES.

**134   (Overleaf) MALE GLASS FROGS
GUARDING EGGS, COSTA RICA**
(Michael and Patricia Fogden)
THE EXTRAORDINARY
TRANSPARENCY OF THESE FROGS
BLENDS THEM WITH THEIR
BACKGROUND AND BLURS THEIR
OUTLINE, CONCEALING THEM
FROM PREDATORS. MALES SIGNAL
TO FEMALES WITH A SYNCOPATED
CHORUS WHICH PENETRATES THE
WALL OF RAINFOREST NOISES.

135

136

**135   CTENUCHID MOTH, COSTA RICA** (Michael and Patricia Fogden)
MASQUERADING AS A POISONOUS ANIMAL IS A COMMON BLUFF EMPLOYED BY
RAINFOREST CREATURES, EFFECTIVELY DETERRING WOULD-BE PREDATORS. THIS
MOTH IS MIMICKING ONE OF THE MOST POISONOUS WASPS IN THE FOREST.

**136   CRAB SPIDER, BRAZIL** (Ken Preston-Mafham/Premaphotos)
CONCEALED AMONG WHITE FLOWERS, THIS SPIDER MIMICS THE PLANTS WITH
SOPHISTICATED CAMOUFLAGE, BUT IT CAN EQUALLY TURN ITS DECEPTIVE
APPEARANCE INTO A PREDATORY DEVICE. ON A BARE BRANCH THE SPIDER
RESEMBLES A FLOWER: UNWARY INSECTS APPROACH TO FEED, ONLY TO BECOME
A MEAL THEMSELVES.

**137   SPIDER MIMICKING ANT, TRINIDAD** (Ken Preston-Mafham/Premaphotos)
DESPITE HAVING EIGHT LEGS, BY WAVING ITS FRONT LEGS AROUND LIKE
ANTENNAE THIS SPIDER PERFECTLY IMITATES AN ANT. ANT-IMITATION IS AN
EXTREMELY SUCCESSFUL STRATEGY AS ANTS, WHICH BITE AND STING AND ARE
OFTEN ACCOMPANIED BY SWARMS OF THEIR COLONY MEMBERS, ARE SOME OF
THE LEAST PREYED UPON ANIMALS IN THE FOREST.

**138   FLAG BUG, PERU**
(Ken Preston-Mafham/Premaphotos)
ADVERTISING A POISONOUS
NATURE IS AN EFFECTIVE DEFENCE
FOR SOME ANIMALS, AND MOST
PREDATORS QUICKLY LEARN TO
RECOGNIZE A PARTICULAR RANGE
OF WARNING COLOUR
COMBINATIONS. THE POISONOUS
FLAG BUG'S LEG IS WARNINGLY
COLOURED, BUT ITS STRATEGY
GOES FURTHER: IF AN
INEXPERIENCED PREDATOR
PERSISTS, IT WAVES ITS VIVID LEG
AROUND TO DISTRACT ATTENTION
FROM ITS BODY. THE DEVICE IS
APPARENTLY SUCCESSFUL, FOR
FLAG BUGS ARE FREQUENTLY SEEN
MISSING ONE OR BOTH LEGS, BUT
OTHERWISE PERFECTLY HEALTHY.

138

**139   GRASSHOPPER, COSTA RICA**
(Ken Preston-Mafham)
THIS GRASSHOPPER NYMPH SHOWS
THE CLASSIC WARNING COLOURS
OF BLACK AND YELLOW, USED BY A
WHOLE RANGE OF INSECTS
INCLUDING EUROPEAN WASPS, A
PATTERN WHICH IMPRINTS ITSELF
FIRMLY ON THE MEMORIES OF
WOULD-BE PREDATORS.

139

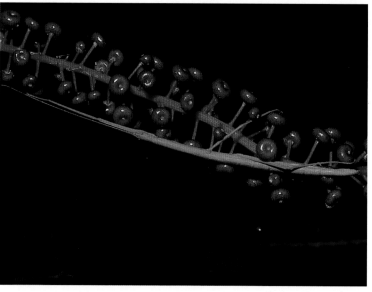

**140   STICK INSECT, COSTA RICA**
(Peter Ward/Bruce Coleman Ltd)
WHETHER GREEN OR BROWN, STICK
INSECTS ARE INDISTINGUISHABLE
FROM THE FOLIAGE ON WHICH
THEY FEED.

140

141 KATYDID 'STARTLE' DISPLAY,
**BRAZIL** (Michael and Patricia Fogden)
THE KATYDID'S SUPERB LEAF
DISGUISE WILL NORMALLY
CONCEAL IT FROM PREDATORS, BUT
SHOULD ONE ATTEMPT TO SEIZE IT,
PERHAPS EVEN BELIEVING IT TO BE
A LEAF, THE KATYDID HAS A LAST
RESORT 'STARTLE' TACTIC, WHEN IT
FLICKS UP A SECOND PAIR OF
DIFFERENTLY COLOURED WINGS.
IN SOME CASES THESE ARE
MARKED WITH SPOTS LIKE EYES,
WHICH MAY SEEM TO THE
PREDATOR LIKE THOSE OF
ANOTHER ANIMAL AND SUCCEED IN
FRIGHTENING IT OFF.

141

142

142 **OWL BUTTERFLY, COSTA RICA**
(Ken Preston-Mafham/Premaphotos)
THE SPECTACULAR 'OWL EYE'
MARKINGS ON THIS BUTTERFLY
MAY SERVE ONE OF SEVERAL
PURPOSES. WHEN DISTURBED, THE
OWL BUTTERFLY LANDS ON A
NEARBY TREE AND DISPLAYS ONLY
ONE 'EYE' TO THE WOULD-BE
PREDATOR: IT MAY BE MIMICKING
THE EYE OF A LARGE PREDATOR,
OR AN UNPALATABLE TREE FROG
WHICH SITS ON TREE TRUNKS.
ALTERNATIVELY, IT MAY BE
DISTRACTING PREDATORS FROM ITS
VULNERABLE BODY: A THEORY
WHICH SEEMS LIKELY AS THESE
BUTTERFLIES ARE OFTEN SEEN
WITH BEAK MARKS SCARRING
THEIR 'OWL EYES'.

143

144

143 **THREE-TOED SLOTH, CENTRAL AMERICA** (Partridge Films) THE LANGUOROUS SLOTH IS FREQUENTLY SEEN IN THE RAINFORESTS OF SOUTH AND CENTRAL AMERICA AND IS ONE OF THE FOREST'S MOST SUCCESSFUL MAMMALS, DESPITE ITS NOTORIOUS LETHARGY. IT SPENDS ITS ENTIRE LIFE IN THE TREE TOPS FEEDING ON LEAVES, DESCENDING ONLY TO URINATE AND DEFECATE ABOUT ONCE A WEEK. IN MOIST CONDITIONS ITS FUR BECOMES COLONIZED BY ALGAE, GIVING IT A GREENISH TINGE WHICH PROBABLY ALSO PROVIDES CAMOUFLAGE. ITS COAT IS ALSO OFTEN HOME TO A MOTH AND SEVERAL KINDS OF BEETLE, WHICH LAY THEIR EGGS IN THE SLOTH'S EXCREMENT WHEN IT DESCENDS TO THE GROUND AND THEN RETURN TO ITS FUR; NEWLY-HATCHED INSECTS FLY INTO THE CANOPY TO FIND THEIR OWN SLOTH HOME.

**144  MANDRILL, WEST CENTRAL AFRICA**

(Rod Williams/Bruce Coleman Ltd)
THE MANDRILL'S FACE HAS
EVOLVED INTO A RIDGED AND
FURROWED, BRIGHTLY COLOURED
MASK, SHAPED INTO A FAKE BUT
PERMANENT SNARL. IN OLDER
MALES, THE SWELLING OF THE
'SNARL' ENLARGES STILL FURTHER,
OFTEN IMPEDING VISION, BUT THE
IMPORTANCE OF GIVING STRONG
VISUAL SIGNALS IN THE DARKNESS
OF THE FOREST UNDERGROWTH
WHERE THE MANDRILL LIVES
OUTWEIGHS EVEN IMPAIRED SIGHT.

**145   BLACK HOWLER MONKEY, SOUTH AMERICA**

(Rod Williams/Bruce Coleman Ltd)
IN THE RAINFOREST, WHERE THE
FIELD OF VISION IS OFTEN
LIMITED, VOCAL SIGNALS CAN BE
AS OR MORE IMPORTANT THAN
VISUAL ONES BETWEEN ANIMALS.
THESE MONKEYS ENGAGE IN
EXTRAORDINARILY LOUD HOWLING
SESSIONS AT DAWN, WHICH ARE A
FORM OF TERRITORIAL DEFENCE.
THE ROAR, WHICH IS
PARTICULARLY LOUD IN THE
MALES, ONCE TERRIFIED
EXPLORERS OF THE NEW WORLD,
WHO MISTOOK IT FOR THE
GROWLING OF JAGUARS.

145

147

146 **MARGAY, BELIZE** (Partridge Films)

147 **JAGUAR PAIR, BELIZE** (Partridge Films)

THE DAPPLED COATS OF THE JUNGLE CATS BLEND PERFECTLY WITH THE LIGHT
ON THE FOREST FLOOR, WHICH SHIFTS AND RIPPLES AS THE FOLIAGE MOVES
ABOVE. UNFORTUNATELY FOR MANY OF THE CATS, PARTICULARLY THE LARGER
JAGUARS AND LEOPARDS, THEIR BEAUTIFUL COATS ARE ALSO DESIRED BY
HUMANS. MANY OF THESE SUPREME RAINFOREST PREDATORS ARE NOW
ENDANGERED THROUGH EXTENSIVE POACHING, WHEN THEY ARE BARBARICALLY
KILLED AND THEIR SKINS ILLEGALLY SOLD. SMALLER CATS, LIKE THE MARGAYS,
ARE NOT USUALLY HUNTED FOR THEIR PELTS, BUT ARE ENDANGERED LIKE MANY
RAINFOREST ANIMALS BY HUNTERS WHO SNARE FOR MEAT, AND THROUGH THE
LOSS OF THEIR HABITAT: THE MARGAY ESPECIALLY SEEMS NOT TO TAKE TO
NEWLY CLEARED AREAS OF FOREST, DESPITE THE ABUNDANCE OF PREY.

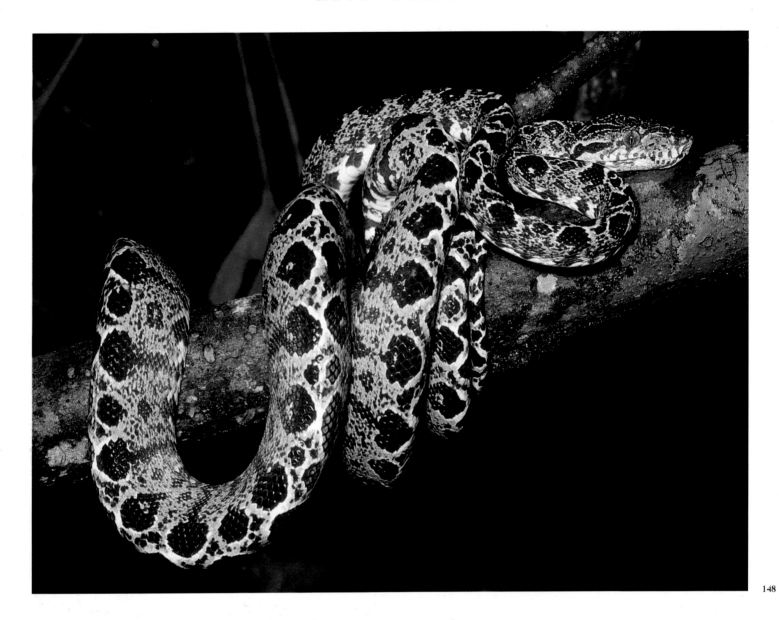

148

**148  TREE BOA, ECUADOR**
(Michael and Patricia Fogden)
THE POWERFUL TREE BOA
STRANGLES ITS PREY – RODENTS,
BIRDS AND THE LIKE – BY
CONSTRICTING ITS MUSCULAR
COILS. DESPITE ITS STRENGTH IT IS
NOT POISONOUS AND THEREFORE
IS VULNERABLE TO PREDATORS
SUCH AS BIRDS OF PREY.

**149  MOTH CATERPILLAR, COSTA
RICA** (Stephen J Krasemann/NHPA)
THIS HARMLESS CATERPILLAR
CONVINCINGLY MIMICS AN
EXTREMELY POISONOUS VIPER
WITH THE UNDERSIDE OF ITS
BODY, SHOWN HERE. IT IS QUITE
LARGE, SO THE DECEPTION IS
CREDIBLE.

149

**150  PARROT SNAKE, COSTA RICA**
(Michael and Patricia Fogden)
A SUPREME BLUFFER, THE PARROT
SNAKE IS NOT VENOMOUS, BUT ITS
VIVID COLOURATION AND
THREATENING POSTURE, WITH
MOUTH GAPING WIDE, IMPLY TO
PREDATORS THAT IT IS.

151

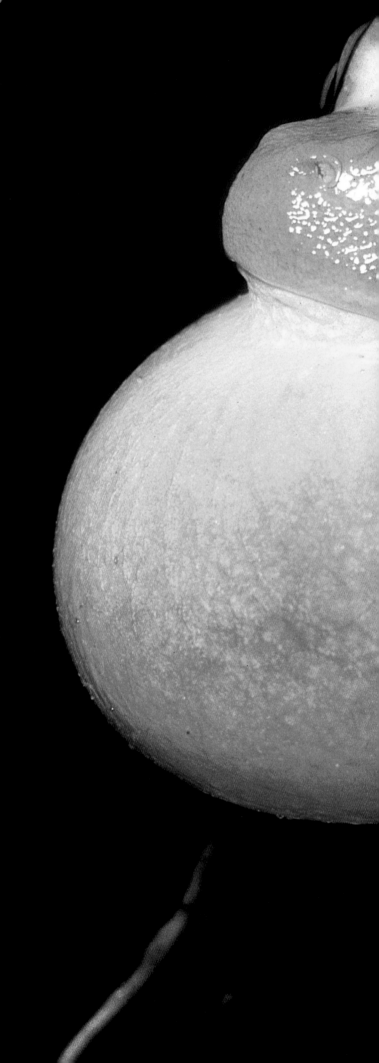

**151 TURQUOISE ARROW-POISON FROG, CENTRAL AMERICA**
(Michael and Patricia Fogden/Bruce Coleman Ltd)
AS ITS NAME SUGGESTS, THE TOXINS IN THIS FROG ARE USED BY
AMERICAN INDIANS TO TIP THEIR ARROWS FOR HUNTING. ALTHOUGH
GREENISH, ITS UNNATURAL, METALLIC COLOURS PROBABLY WARN
PREDATORS OF ITS INEDIBLE NATURE, RATHER THAN CAMOUFLAGING IT.

**152 CHAMELEON, MADAGASCAR** (Ken Preston-Mafham/Premaphotos)
THE CHAMELEON'S COLORATION DOES NOT, CONTRARY TO MYTH,
CHANGE TO MATCH ITS SURROUNDINGS – THE RESPONSE IS, IN FACT,
TO TEMPERATURE.

**153 RED EYED TREE FROG, AUSTRALIA** (Ken Preston-Mafham/Premaphotos)
BY NIGHT, THE MALES OF THIS SPECIES GATHER TOGETHER TO
ATTRACT FEMALES BY CALLING IN A LOUD AND RESONANT CHORUS
THROUGH THE FOREST. SUCH MALE COURTING GROUPS ARE KNOWN AS
LEKS AND ARE COMMON AMONG BIRDS, FROGS AND BUTTERFLIES.

152

154

155

156

154    **BLACK-NECKED RED COTINGA, PERU** (Michael and Patricia Fogden)

155    **BOWERBIRD, AUSTRALIA** (Leo Meier/Weldon Trannies)

156    **SCARLET MACAWS, SOUTH AMERICA** (Gunter Ziesler/Bruce Coleman Ltd)
RAINFOREST BIRDS DISPLAY THE MOST ASTONISHING PLUMAGES, WHICH ARE
USED FOR IDENTIFICATION AND COMMUNICATION BETWEEN MEMBERS OF THE
SAME SPECIES. THIS IS PARTICULARLY IN EVIDENCE DURING COURTSHIP, AS THIS
MALE RED COTINGA DISPLAYING TO A FEMALE SHOWS (154). IN THE CASE OF
PARROTS AND MACAWS (SEEN HERE SCRAPING THE ROCK TO FIND SALT),
DIFFERENT COLORATION PATTERNS MAY HELP SPECIES DISTINCTION.

# CHAPTER SEVEN

# BETWEEN THE TREES – THE CANOPY COMMUNITY
## Andrew Mitchell

*The trees create the framework for the forest, in both evolutionary and physical terms. Their leaves, fruit and flowers, even their twigs and resin, support a multitude of animals, many of which live among their branches high in the canopy and are never or only rarely seen. More surprisingly, there are also a whole host of plants which depend on the trees for their survival - for their access to energy-giving sunlight, even for their nutrition. These plants in turn are home to a vast array of smaller animals, inconspicuous beside the bright birds and the monkeys which dart and leap through the branches, but which also make up the life of this canopy community.*

FROM THE DIM FLOOR OF THE RAINFOREST, THE CANOPY appears as a jungle of interlocking branches and tree limbs draped with lianas. In fact, it is a complex network of arboreal highways leading through a maze of spaces, hollows and niches, providing a wide variety of habitats for the myriad creatures which inhabit it.

The architecture of individual trees provides the solid matrix for all other life in the forest. Some, the emergents, grow to tremendous heights. Beneath them nestle other lesser trees which form the continuous leaf layer of the canopy, and below these again trees with oblong crowns fit between the massive trunks of the emergents. Larger animals swing and scamper along familiar pathways through the canopy with nonchalant ease.

The ability to move with such confidence in the forest is the product of millions of years of co-evolution between animals and plants. Many mammals, such as monkeys, have powerful

---

**157 TREE WITH EPIPHYTES, QUEENSLAND, AUSTRALIA** (Leo Meier/Weldon Trannies)
THERE ARE FEW SPACES BETWEEN OR ON THE TREES IN THE RAINFOREST WHICH ARE NOT COLONIZED. PLANTS HANG AND TWIST AND CLIMB AND CREEP ON TREES AT EVERY LEVEL FROM FOREST FLOOR TO CANOPY: SOME BENEFIT THE TREE WHICH IS THEIR HOST, BUT OTHERS SUCK ITS NUTRIENTS, STRANGLE OR SHADE IT OR WEIGH IT DOWN SO HEAVILY THAT IT DIES. AMONG THE LIANAS WHICH TRAIL AND THE EPIPHYTIC PLANTS WHICH CLING, ALMOST ROOTLESS, TO THE TRUNK AND BRANCHES OF THE TREE, LIVE A MULTITUDE OF CREATURES WHICH MAY NEVER TOUCH THE GROUND.

limbs with which to bridge the gap between trees in their search for food. Some lizards and squirrels cross gaps on membranes of skin. Some frogs glide short distances on parachutes of skin stretched between their toes, and in Borneo there is even a species of snake which floats through the air, flattening its body aerodynamically. Throughout the night bats fly along tunnels formed by overhanging branches of green leaves, and by day birds twist and weave through every part of the forest on iridescent, multi-coloured wings. The forest also provides regions of varying humidity and light which flying insects inhabit: dragonflies, mayflies, midges and gnats hover here on flashing wings, and spiders cast their webs to catch passing flies. Giant damselflies float through these gaps like miniature helicopters on four independently beating wings, searching for the webs of saucer-sized orb-weaving spiders. Mesmerized by the damselfly's wings, the spider makes no attempt to escape. In an instant the damselfly seizes the spider and makes off with it, snapping the thorax and sending its head and legs spinning to earth, saving only the juicy abdomen to be devoured.

Not all inhabitants of the spaces between the trees are animals. Many are botanical hitch-hikers seeking a place in the sun. To gain access to energy-producing light in the canopy, plants without strong stems must either keep their roots in the ground and grow up tall trees, as do lianas and vines, or they must abandon the earth altogether and, with the help of flying animals or the wind, colonize the branches. Some plants produce lightweight seeds which float up into the canopy, while other seeds pass through the guts of birds which deposit them there. Mistletoes have sticky seeds which adhere to the tail feathers of the flowerpeckers which eat them. The birds then skitter up and down branches, rubbing their bottoms on the bark to be rid of the seeds, so forcing them into woody crevices where they can germinate. Mistletoes draw sustenance from the hosts they parasitize, but another group of plants use branches merely to gain a foothold in the most productive part of the forest, and have become so successful that they all but dominate the environment there. These are the epiphytes.

Epiphytes, or air plants as they are sometimes known, comprise some 28,000 species in sixty-five families, most of which occur in the great rainforests of America and South East Asia. In America bromeliads are also to be found, along with arboreal cacti, orchids, ferns, mosses, liverworts and lichens. Even the surface of an individual leaf may sprout a veritable jungle of micro-epiphytes just millimetres high. The weight of all these epiphytes in a tree crown can reach several tonnes.

Only in recent years has the true importance of epiphytes to the rainforest community been realized. Epiphytes are faced with the dual perils of starvation and dehydration. Although rainforests are among the world's wettest habitats, the canopy is a dry place. Many epiphytes therefore exhibit characteristics similar to those of desert plants. Bromeliads, which are related to pineapples, have evolved into water tanks. Their spiky leaves channel water into the centre of the plant, which may hold as much as ten litres (eighteen pints). It also captures falling leaves, which rot, thus providing nutrients which the bromeliad cannot retrieve from the soil. Many other epiphytes also obtain nutrients in this way.

Bromeliads provide drinking water for passing monkeys and lizards, and a place to lay eggs for giant damselflies and mosquitoes, the former eating the latter as they hatch into aquatic larvae. A single bromeliad has been known to contain four harvestmen, a tiny spider brooding over some eggs, three different kinds of woodlice, a centipede, a jumping millipede, a pseudoscorpion, various metallic beetles, earwigs, a tree seedling in an advanced stage of germination, some chironomid fly larvae, a nest of ants, an earthworm, mites galore and a small frog.

Far from being a burden, many epiphytes are of great benefit to trees. The leaves, bird droppings and decaying bodies of creatures which have used them as their homes combine to form a valuable source of nutrients high above ground. In addition, fine hairs on epiphyte leaves trap nutrients from dust particles in the air or dissolved in rain. Fully half of all the nutrients in the rainforest canopy foliage may be spirited out of the air and locked up into epiphytes in this way. Trees have turned this to their own advantage, sending roots from their branches into the mineral-rich epiphyte garden to pirate its nutrients before it falls to the ground. So finely balanced is this scramble for scarce food that some trees grow roots into their own trunks or those of neighbouring trees to tap their rotting cores. Most canopy giants are in fact hollow. A woodpecker hole may be widened to allow a host of other creatures to live inside. The droppings or prey of bats, snakes and owls serve to enrich further the tree's meagre food supply, so giving it an advantage over its neighbours.

The evolution of such relationships between plants and animals and between plants and other plants is one of the most absorbing fields of study in rainforests. Ants are to be found at almost every level in rainforests: many trees have hollow branches infested with them, their role being to protect the tree from defoliating predators in return for their secure home. Such mutually beneficial partnerships between ants and plants are commonplace in the tropics.

Most fascinating of all are the ways in which bromeliads are used as tadpole nurseries by certain tropical frogs. In the dimly lit interior of the forest in Central America, tiny arrow poison frogs, which would comfortably sit on a penny piece, embark on quite extraordinary journeys to ensure the care of their young. After the tadpoles hatch in a small burrow in the ground they wriggle on to the female's back, and she begins a prodigious climb up a tree trunk in search of a bromeliad filled with water. On finding one high above ground she will reverse into it, dropping the tadpoles into the water, each into a separate leaf axil where, safe from ground predators, the tadpoles feed on algae and mosquito larvae. Each day the female returns and reverses again into the bromeliad to touch the water surface. If a tadpole is present it vibrates the water surface with its tail and signals to its mother to release a single unfertilized egg – a food parcel to ensure its survival.

A young canopy tree bound for the forest roof must run the gauntlet of clinging vines and lianas which seek to hitch a ride there too. Some take evasive action: pioneer species which rely on rapid growth to colonize light gaps periodically slough off their bark, perhaps to rid themselves of other hindering plants. Some lianas will outlive the tree in which they grow, rising again into the tree tops on a young tree after their original host has fallen. More remarkable still are the strangling figs. These extraordinary plants begin their life as a tiny seed deposited in the branches of a canopy tree. As the plant grows it sends down roots which on reaching the ground thicken rapidly, sucking moisture and goodness from the earth. Eventually, the strangling fig's branches shade out its host's leaves and encase its trunk in a coffin of roots. Gradually, the host's trunk rots away, leaving a massive hollow lattice of roots belonging to the strangler alone. From such death, new abundance is born because the strangling fig is one of the most prolific fruiting trees in the forest and a whole host of creatures flock to its branches to gorge themselves on figs. This arboreal feast has only one purpose from the fig tree's point of view – to disperse its seeds to fertile places in which new strangling figs may grow. It is no mystery that syrup of figs is a laxative. Fig trees evolved that way to ensure their seeds come through unscathed.

Fortunately, the unusual hollow trunk of the strangling fig confers a benefit which no Darwinian evolutionist could have foreseen. Its numerous tough roots make the mature tree difficult and dangerous to fell even with a chainsaw, bulldozer or axe. After loggers have passed, the *Matapalo*, or death-tree as the strangling fig is sometimes known, is often the only species left standing, a forlorn island of hope for the forest's survivors, in a wasteland of fallen trees.

**159 BROMELIADS GROWING ON TREE, BRAZIL** (Luiz Claudio Marigo) PLANTS OF THE BROMELIAD FAMILY, WHICH WE FREQUENTLY SEE AS HOUSEPLANTS, OFTEN GROW AS EPIPHYTES IN THE COOL AND ULTRA-HUMID MONTANE FORESTS OF SOUTH AMERICA. EPIPHYTES ARE PLANTS WHICH HAVE GAINED ACCESS TO THE SUN WITHOUT HAVING TO EXPEND ENERGY BY GROWING TRUNKS, STEMS OR ROOTS WHICH TAP INTO THE GROUND. INSTEAD, THEIR SEEDS LODGE IN CREVICES AND CRACKS HIGH IN A TREE AND THERE THEY GROW, SUCKING MOISTURE AND NUTRIENT PARTICLES FROM THE AIR, SOMETIMES STEALING NOURISHMENT FROM THEIR HOST PLANT OR GATHERING FOREST DEBRIS AMONG THEIR LEAVES FOR THEIR OWN FOOD STORE.

159

160

160　RED-BILLED SCYTHE BILL,
BRAZIL (Luiz Claudio Marigo)
THIS SCYTHE BILL IS, LIKE THE
HUMMINGBIRDS, A NECTAR
FEEDER. DARTING AMONG THE
TREES, IT FREQUENTLY FEEDS ON
THE NECTAR OF THE BRIGHTLY
COLOURED BROMELIAD FLOWERS,
WHICH SHINE LIKE BEACONS
AMONG THE DENSE FOREST
FOLIAGE.

161

161　BROMELIADS AND OTHER
EPIPHYTES, BLUE MOUNTAINS,
JAMAICA (Michael and Patricia Fogden)
HIGH IN THE CANOPY, THE
ROTTING LEAVES AND INSECTS
TRAPPED BY THE LEAVES OF BROAD
SPIKY EPIPHYTES, PARTICULARLY
BROMELIADS, CAN BECOME A
USEFUL SOURCE OF NUTRITION
FOR THE HOST TREE. SOME GROW
ROOTS INTO 'THEIR' EPIPHYTES,
PIRATING THE GATHERED
NUTRIENTS FOR THEIR OWN
BENEFIT.

162

163

**167  PYGMY MARSUPIAL FROG,
CENTRAL AMERICA**
(Michael Fogden/Bruce Coleman Ltd)
THESE TINY MARSUPIAL FROGS ARE
RELATIVELY EASY TO FIND SITTING
AMONG THE LEAVES. THIS FEMALE
HAS HAD HER FERTLIZED EGGS
PLACED IN THE SAC UNDER THE
SKIN ON HER BACK BY HER MATE
WHERE THEY WILL MATURE, TO
TADPOLE STAGE, AT THIS POINT
SHE TIPS THEM INTO A WATER
POOL TO FINISH THEIR
DEVELOPMENT.

167

**168  RED AND BLUE POISON-
ARROW FROG**
(Michael Fogden/Bruce Coleman Ltd)

**169  RETICULATED POISON-ARROW
FROG, PERU**
(Michael and Patricia Fogden)
MANY OF THE POISON-ARROW
FROGS LAY THEIR EGGS ON LAND,
AFTER WHICH THE EGGS ARE
GUARDED, USUALLY BY THE MALE
BUT SOMETIMES BY THE FEMALE,
UNTIL THEY HATCH. THE NEW
TADPOLES THEN WRIGGLE ONTO
THE BACK OF THE FEMALE, WHO
BEGINS A LONG CLIMB INTO THE
CANOPY. HER MISSION IS TO FIND A
BROMELIAD FILLED WITH WATER,
INTO WHICH SHE CAREFULLY
DROPS EACH TADPOLE. THE
TADPOLES WILL MATURE INTO
FROGS IN THE BROMELIAD POOL,
NURTURED BY THE MOTHER, WHO
CONTINUES TO PROVIDE FOOD FOR
THEM ON DAILY VISITS.

168

169

**170  RED-EYED LEAF FROGS, COSTA
RICA** (Michael and Patricia Fogden)
RED-EYED LEAF FROGS, OR GAUDY
FROGS AS THEY ARE ALSO,
UNDERSTANDABLY, KNOWN, SPEND
MANY OF THE DAYTIME HOURS IN
BROMELIAD POOLS OR SITTING ON
A GREEN LEAF. BREEDING TAKES
PLACE BY NIGHT, BEGINNING WHEN
THE FEMALE ANSWERS A 'CLUCK'
FROM A NEARBY MALE. SHE MAY
LAY SEVERAL CLUTCHES OF EGGS
IN ONE NIGHT. SHOWN HERE IS
THE MALE MATING WITH THE
MUCH LARGER FEMALE; BUT A
SECOND MALE (SEEN ABOVE) IS
TRYING TO CLAIM THE RIGHT
AS HIS.

171 **CERCROPIA TREE: PROTEIN-GIVING BODIES PROVIDED FOR ANTS, COSTA RICA**

(Ken Preston-Mafham/Premaphotos)

172 **CERCROPIA TREE: LEAVES, COSTA RICA**

(Ken Preston-Mafham/Premaphotos)

THE ANTS WHICH INHABIT THE HOLLOW BRANCHES OF THE CERCROPIA TREE FARM SAP-SUCKING SCALE INSECTS FOR THE HONEYDEW THEY EXCRETE; THE SCALE INSECTS' DEBT TO THE ANTS IS THAT THEY CANNOT PIERCE THE BARK WITHOUT THEM. THE TREE IS REWARDED FOR ITS HOSPITALITY BY THE ANTS, WHO DEFEND IT FROM PREDATORS BY VIGOROUSLY STINGING THEM. TO FURTHER ENCOURAGE ITS GUARDIANS THE TREE PRODUCES PROTEIN-RICH CAPSULES (171) AT THE BASE OF ITS

LEAVES AND NECTAR FROM ITS LEAVES. THE INTACT LEAVES SHOWN HERE ARE CHARACTERISTIC OF ANT-PROTECTED TREES: CERCROPIAS ARE NOT CHEMICALLY DEFENDED AND THE LEAVES OF TREES WITHOUT ANTS SHOW CONSIDERABLE DAMAGE.

171

172

166

173

**173  DISCHIDIA VINE, SOUTH EAST ASIA** (Ken Preston-Mafham/Premaphotos)
THE DISCHIDIA VINE GROWS THESE HANGING COMPARTMENTS WHICH ARE
COLONIZED BY ANTS. THE ANTS BRING IN DECAYING DEBRIS AND BY SENDING
ROOTS INTO THE COMPARTMENTS THE VINE OBTAINS NUTRIENTS.

**174  GREEN TREE ANTS, AUSTRALIA** (Ken Preston-Mafham/Premaphotos)
THESE TREE ANTS MAKE THEIR NESTS FROM LEAVES WHICH THEY INGENIOUSLY
MESH TOGETHER: AN ANT LARVA IS GENTLY SQUEEZED BY ONE OF THE WORKERS
LIKE A TUBE OF TOOTHPASTE UNTIL IT EXUDES A STICKY SILK SUBSTANCE, WHICH
IS USED TO 'SEW' THE FABRIC OF THE LEAF NEST. THE SAME SPECIES OF
'WEAVING' ANTS ALSO OCCUR IN SOUTH EAST ASIA AND CENTRAL AFRICA.

174

**175  RED COLOBUS, GAMBIA**
(Stephen Dalton/NHPA)

**176  BLACK SPIDER MONKEY, PERU**
(Gunter Ziesler/Bruce Coleman Ltd)
FOR THE AGILE MONKEYS OF THE
CANOPY, THE INTERLOCKED TREES
AND MESHED LIANAS WAY ABOVE
THE GROUND FORM WELL-KNOWN
PATHWAYS WHICH ARE IN
CONSTANT USE. THERE IS LITTLE
NEED FOR EITHER OF THESE
MONKEYS EVER TO DESCEND TO
THE FOREST FLOOR. SPIDER
MONKEYS ARE INCREDIBLY
RELAXED IN THE TREE TOPS: AGILE
AND MOBILE, THEY USE THEIR
TAILS AS A FIFTH LIMB WHICH
PERMITS ENDLESS VARIATION OF
MOVEMENT. THE LARGE RED
COLOBUS IS ALSO A FOREST
ACROBAT CAPABLE OF
SPECTACULAR LEAPS, BUT IS FAR
LESS ENERGETIC THAN THE SPIDER
MONKEY. THE REASON LIES IN THE
RESPECTIVE DIGESTIVE SYSTEMS
OF THE SPECIES: THE SPIDER
MONKEY EATS ENERGY-RICH,
EASILY DIGESTED FRUIT, WHEREAS
THE COLOBUS EATS ALMOST
EXCLUSIVELY LEAVES. THESE IT
DIGESTS IN A DOUBLE STOMACH,
RATHER LIKE AN AERIAL COW:
SUCH DIGESTION TAKES TIME,
HENCE THE COLOBUS' LAZIER
LIFESTYLE.

175

176

**177  RUFOUS MOUSE LEMUR,
MADAGASCAR**
(Ken Preston-Mafham/Premaphotos)
AMONG THE SMALLEST OF ALL THE
PRIMATES, THE MOUSE LEMUR
SCURRIES THROUGH THE TREES
WITH SOME AGILITY. BY DAY,
GROUPS OF UP TO FIFTEEN
FEMALES AND YOUNG LEMURS
SLEEP IN NESTS BUILT IN DENSE
FOLIAGE OR IN HOLES IN TREES; BY
NIGHT THEY DISPERSE TO FORAGE,
PARTICULARLY FOR FRUIT.

179

**179 PITCHER PLANT, MADAGASCAR**
(O. Langrand/Bruce Coleman Ltd)
PITCHERS ARE AMONG THE
RELATIVELY FEW CARNIVOROUS
PLANTS IN THE WORLD: THEY TRAP,
DROWN AND DIGEST INSECTS IN
THEIR LIQUID-FILLED PITCHERS.
MANY CARNIVOROUS INSECTS ALSO
EXPLOIT THE PITCHER'S ABILITIES,
AND FEED ON THE DEAD AND
DYING INSECTS: TWENTY-SEVEN
SPECIES WERE RECORDED IN ONE
KIND OF PITCHER. ALTHOUGH
USUALLY A PLANT OF SOUTH-EAST
ASIAN FORESTS, THIS SPECIES IS
ENDEMIC TO MADAGASCAR.

**178 CLIMBING PEPPER VINE,
BORNEO**
(Ken Preston-Mafham/Premaphotos)
NON-WOODY CLIMBING PLANTS
SUCH AS THIS PEPPER ARE
COMMON IN THE FOREST,
PARTICULARLY IN MORE OPEN
AREAS WITH PLENTY OF LIGHT,
WHERE THE VINES CAN FORM A
VERITABLE BLANKET OVER THE
VEGETATION. LIKE ALL THE
CLIMBERS AND THE EPIPHYTES,
THEIR GAIN IS THAT THEY SAVE
ENERGY BY RELYING ON ANOTHER
PLANT FOR SUPPORT.

178

180

**180 STRANGLING FIG: QUEENSLAND, AUSTRALIA** (Kathie Atkinson/OSF)
STRANGLING FIGS GROW IN TROPICAL FORESTS ALL OVER THE WORLD, STARTING
AS TINY SEEDS LODGED IN THE RAINFOREST CANOPY. THE TINY PLANT GROWS
ON ITS HOST UNTIL IT IS LARGE ENOUGH TO SEND DOWN LONG ROOTS TO THE
GROUND, WHERE THEY SUCK UP NUTRIENTS AND WATER. THE ROOTS THICKEN
AND SOLIDIFY, EVENTUALLY BECOMING TRUNK-LIKE IN SIZE. BY THIS TIME THE
FIG HAS ABSORBED THE NUTRIENTS DESTINED FOR THE ORIGINAL TREE AND
SHADED IT FROM THE SUN IT NEEDS FOR GROWTH; THE TREE DIES AND FINALLY
ROTS AWAY, LEAVING A HOLLOW FIG TREE WHOSE TRUNK IS A NETWORK OF
ENORMOUS WOODY ROOTS.

*CHAPTER EIGHT*

# FROM DEATH INTO LIFE –
# THE NEVERENDING CYCLE
## Professor David Bellamy

*In the rainforest more than in any other environment, death is the source of new life. Dead leaves, wood, flowers and insects fall in a continuous rain from the trees, littering the forest floor; occasionally the body of a larger animal is also seen. But nothing lies there for long: every scrap of debris is rapidly processed by a multitude of micro-organisms, plants and animals known as the decomposers. These feed on the dead matter, breaking it down so that ultimately almost every one of its useful molecules is made available for use by the green plants which are the basis of life in the forest. This highly efficient system of recycling helps to explain the luxuriance of tropical forests: for the paradox is that its abundant growth rests, in nearly every case, on soils which are acid and poor in nutrients.*

Rainforests are by definition dominated by trees, each one of which is a sophisticated chemical factory, combining the energy of the sun, the rainwater that gives the forests their name, and carbon dioxide from the atmosphere in the process of photosynthesis. The product is energy – essential for fuelling the trees' growth, and for the manufacture of a whole gamut of complex biochemicals – sugars, amino acids, proteins, cellulose, tannins, lignins, fats, waxes, hormones, drugs and fragrances, to name but a few. Many a multinational company would be proud to list such a range on their catalogues – but no industrial complex yet designed by humans could produce anything like such a variety and number of biochemical products using so few resources, on such economically arranged premises, and with no harmful wastes or by-products.

It must be admitted, however, that trees are the world's number one litter louts, for there is really no such thing as a truly

---

**181  FALLEN SANDRAGON LEAF, PUERTO RICO** (Gerry Ellis/Ellis Wildlife Collection) ON THE DARK FLOOR OF THE FOREST LIES THE KEY TO ITS RICHNESS. A THIN LAYER OF DEAD PLANT AND ANIMAL MATTER HOLDS ALL THE NUTRIENTS WHICH ARE AVAILABLE FOR UPTAKE BY THE FOREST PLANTS, BUT FIRST THEY MUST BE BROKEN DOWN INTO MANAGEABLE FRAGMENTS. ALMOST AS SOON AS A DEAD LEAF OR INSECT LANDS, A WHOLE HOST OF DECOMPOSERS BEGIN PROCESSING THE MATERIAL, SHREDDING, CHEWING, DIGESTING AND ABSORBING, RECLAIMING THE NUTRIENTS WHICH CAN THEN BE USED BY NEW FOREST GROWTH.

evergreen leaf. Each one must eventually come to the end of its productive life and fall to the ground. But even before it reaches it, each and every one of the biochemicals it contains is scheduled for use, and its components for recycling, by a complex and fantastic web of organisms known as the decomposers. These encompass a complete cross-section of all the four main kingdoms of living things: the prokaryotes, which include bacteria and blue-green algae; the fungi, including mushrooms, toadstools, yeasts, moulds and slime moulds; the green plants such as algae; and the animals, from single-celled protists to mammals. The forest seethes with them: millions upon millions of individuals in every square metre, each with a vital job to perform – and each deserving the distinction of a latin name, although to date fewer than one per cent have been granted such human recognition.

The rainforest is a perfectly balanced, self-sufficient system which depends on recycling for its very existence. Each leaf on every tree in the forest has a life story so intricate and subtly balanced that it may serve as a key to understanding the superb economy of the rainforest ecosystem.

Every leaf starts its life as a group of cells cut off in the living apex of a stem, a bud which will one day unfold into a green powerhouse. Growth of the young leaf may be so rapid that its size outstrips the capacity of the system to strengthen the new tissue, so it hangs limp. It may be suffused with red pigments to protect the delicate chlorophyll from too much sunlight, which could damage it in its nascent state. At this stage, leaves are very tender and ultra vulnerable to insect attack; many are likely to be eaten. A leaf growing on a myrmecophyte, however, will be well protected – by insect 'vigilantes'. Myrmecophytes are trees which live in a state of symbiosis – of mutual help – with colonies of ants. The tree provides the ants with a home and a food source, and they in return defend the tree, their habitat, from attack by other living things. The arrangement suits both parties perfectly.

The leaves which survive often develop a thick cuticle to minimize water loss at times of stress and a 'drip tip' to channel rain quickly from the lamina. Some leaves also have special motor cells at their base: and so begins their life as part of the photosynthetic machinery of the forest. The motor cells allow the leaf to turn, orientating its green solar cells in relation to the direction and intensity of the sun. High in the canopy, under the full force of the tropical sun, the leaf could overheat and die; so it turns its edge to the incident radiation. Yet should clouds obscure the sun, the leaf will again turn face up; and if growing in the dark lower layers of the forest it will angle itself so as to absorb as many as possible of the diffuse rays which straggle through the canopy of trees.

The remarkable opportunism of this adaptation for rapid on/off photosynthesis shows how the leaf's whole structure, cellular anatomy and life chemistry is geared towards seizing every chance and making full use of it, while at the same time minimizing stress and damage. This is an overriding concern, for once the system is impaired in any way, the teeming hordes of disease and decay-promoting organisms which have waited for just such a moment will waste no time in seizing their own opportunity.

On a day to day basis, the intake and uptake of both carbon dioxide and oxygen are in quasi equilibrium, both within the forest ecosystem and within the atmosphere which is shared by all life on earth. Rainforests do not recharge the atmosphere with oxygen, nor do they deplete its carbon dioxide reserves, but the living mass – trunks, branches, leaves, plants and animals – holds a lot of carbon in store. And when burned, carbon becomes carbon dioxide – a potent greenhouse gas. As the forest is destroyed, so is the balance in the earth's atmosphere, for great amounts of carbon dioxide are released into the air, contributing to the potentially devastating greenhouse effect.

This gigantic carbon store is anchored by living roots which secure the trees and bind the soil, holding it and a vast reservoir of water in place. This water is drawn on day and night by the trees to supply the life process of each leaf. Some of it is used as a raw material for photosynthesis, while the excess evaporates from the leaves, keeping them cool and saturating the air above with water vapour. Insulated by the canopy, the forest is thus a living mist unit, ameliorating the tropical climate, keeping desertification at bay – and on a broader scale helping to control local, regional and even global climates. These are just some of the functions of the world's tropical rainforests and their many billions of leaves.

The life of every one of these leaves eventually draws to a close. In preparation for the loss of a leaf, the tree draws back key minerals like phosphates, nitrates, potassium and others which are in short supply into temporary store in the living trunk. Supplies of water, salts and sugars are then shut off from the dying leaf, which is loosened ready to be blown away. After a few brief moments of freedom floating down through the canopy, each leaf immediately becomes part of the decomposing and recycling chain of life. Once it is on the ground, a whole shade-living community of fungi and bacteria locks in on the leaf's potential, penetrating and softening its now decaying tissues. All manner of insects and other creeping crawling things join in the process, which will eventually make use of every last calorie of energy and recycle every last molecule of nutrient.

Fungi are the key to this leak-proof and magically efficient recycling system. We only become aware of them when their fruiting bodies – toadstools, puffballs, and the like – form to bear the spores up into the light of day, but the whole forest floor is enmeshed with a weft of their microscopic, hair-like hypahe, the form in which they spend most of their lives. Fungi do not photosynthesize but feed by digesting dead organic matter with special enzymes, and in the process release nutrients for use by other plants. Particularly essential to the ecosystem are the mycorrhizal fungi, which weave their threads into a mat around and even inside the roots of the canopy trees, feeding from the sugar and nitrogen containing substances within. In return, the roots take up from the fungi the minerals it has absorbed from the debris of the forest. Thus the greatest and the least of the forest's plants are linked in a symbiotic association which from death and decay produces fresh growth and new life.

So the continuous rain of death from above – leaves, twigs and flowers – along with the carcasses of animals great and small are transformed by the decomposers into components which can be reused by the green plants, the base of the forest food chain. There is no room for waste, for if the cycle of the rainforest is broken, the precious minerals will leach out and the rain will carry them away. The living soil, already sour and impoverished, will no longer be able to support all the wonder of the forest.

Thus the rainforest recycles itself, making no demands on the rest of the environment. Yet its every hectare contributes to the rest of the world, both in terms of the materials it provides and by performing a vital function within the balance of nature: and the most remarkable thing is that in its natural state it costs not one penny piece, not a single calorie of fossil or atomic fuel, nor gramme of non-renewable resource to maintain.

Nevertheless, one million hectares are being destroyed each month: a million hectares of the system which gives life to at least half of all the sorts of plants and animals on earth. At the present rate of destruction, within forty years there will be no large areas left. Climates are changing, deserts are expanding, and already people are suffering. By the end of this sad century more than one million rainforest species will have been forced into extinction and one third of all the world's arable and pastoral land will have become semi-desert. The global consequences of rainforest destruction are far more terrible in their implications even than a limited atomic war. This destruction must be stopped now before it is too late.

---

**182 SNAIL ON BAMBOO, PUERTO RICO** (Gerry Ellis/Ellis Wildlife Collection)
PLANTS CONTAIN BASIC NUTRIENTS, SOME OF WHICH CANNOT BE
MANUFACTURED BY ANIMALS. HERBIVOROUS ANIMALS RELY ON PLANTS FIRST TO
PROCESS THE NUTRIENTS, WHICH THEY THEN ABSORB 'SECOND HAND', READY-
CONVERTED FOR THEIR USE. THESE HERBIVORES ARE THEN EATEN IN THEIR
TURN BY THE CARNIVORES. THUS THE NUTRIENTS ARE IN ACTIVE SERVICE ALL
ALONG THE FOOD CHAIN, FROM THE TINIEST SEEDLING TO THE LARGEST
CARNIVORE.

183

**183   LEAF-CUTTER ANTS, COSTA RICA** (Ken Preston-Mafham/Premaphotos)
LEAF-CUTTER ANTS, COMMON THROUGHOUT TROPICAL AMERICA, BREAK DOWN
HUGE AMOUNTS OF VEGETATION. THE PIECES OF LEAVES – AND SOMETIMES
FLOWERS – ARE TAKEN BACK TO THEIR UNDERGROUND NESTS, WHERE THEY ARE
FURTHER SHREDDED AND PROCESSED BY WORKERS, AND FINALLY SOWN WITH
FUNGAL SPORES. THE RESULTING FUNGUS GARDENS PROVIDE THE ANTS WITH
FOOD.

**184   LEAF SKELETON ON LIVERWORT, PUERTO RICO** (Gerry Ellis/Ellis Wildlife Collection)

**185   CRABCLAW TREE BLOSSOMS, PUERTO RICO** (Gerry Ellis/Ellis Wildlife Collection)

**186   LEAVES IN WATER, AUSTRALIA** (Leo Meier/Weldon Trannies)

**187   POINSETTIA LEAVES, PUERTO RICO** (Gerry Ellis)
EACH LEAF WHICH DROPS TO THE GROUND IN THE RAINFOREST BECOMES PART
OF THE LEAF LITTER, A THIN LAYER OF ORGANIC MATERIAL IN VARYING STAGES
OF DECOMPOSITION. THESE LEAVES WILL SOON BE UNRECOGNIZABLE: THE RATE
OF PRODUCTION IN THE FOREST, FUELLED BY LIGHT, HEAT AND DAMP, IS
ENORMOUSLY FAST. IT IS KEPT IN DYNAMIC BALANCE BY AN EQUALLY
PRODIGIOUS RATE OF DECOMPOSITION.

184

185

186

187

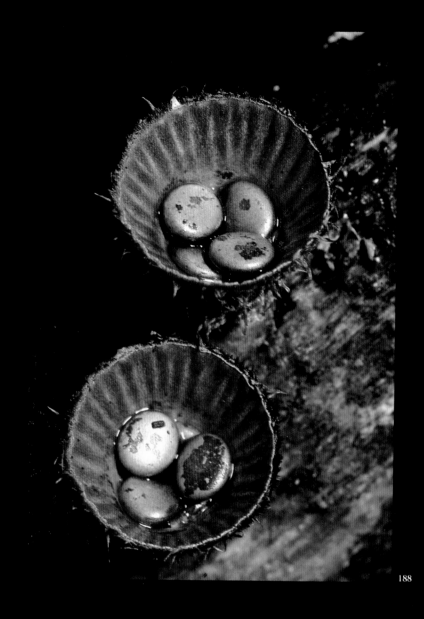

188

188   BIRD'S NEST FUNGUS, COSTA RICA (Michael and Patricia Fogden)

189   CUP FUNGUS, COSTA RICA (Michael and Patricia Fogden)

190   STARFISH FUNGUS, PAPUA NEW GUINEA
(C & D Frith/Bruce Coleman Ltd)

FUNGI OF A MULTITUDE OF SHAPES, SIZES AND COLOURS DECOMPOSE MUCH
RAINFOREST DEBRIS. LIVING AS THEY DO ON THE SUNLESS FOREST FLOOR, THEY
CANNOT GAIN ENERGY FROM SUNLIGHT AND PHOTOSYNTHESIS; INSTEAD THEY
FEED ON DEAD ORGANIC MATTER, BREAKING IT DOWN SIMULTANEOUSLY. MOST
OF THEIR LIVES THEY EXIST ONLY AS TINY THREADS WHICH PENETRATE PLANT
TISSUE AND SECRETE SUBSTANCES TO BREAK DOWN THE TISSUES IN ORDER TO
OBTAIN FOOD FOR GROWTH. IN CERTAIN CONDITIONS, A CLUSTER OF THESE
THREADS FORM WHAT WE KNOW AS A TOADSTOOL, WHICH PRODUCES
REPRODUCTIVE SPORES.

189

190

191

**191 PARASOL FUNGUS, COSTA RICA** (Michael and Patricia Fogden)
THESE TINY PARASOLS MEASURE ONLY 6MM(¼IN ACROSS. DAVID BELLAMY SAW
THEM USED BY THE AUKA INDIANS OF THE AMAZON FOREST TO CURE
DIARRHOEA IN INFANTS. A PASTE MADE FROM THE FUNGI WAS SPREAD ON THE
MOTHER'S BREAST AND FED TO HER BABY, WITH IMPRESSIVE RESULTS.

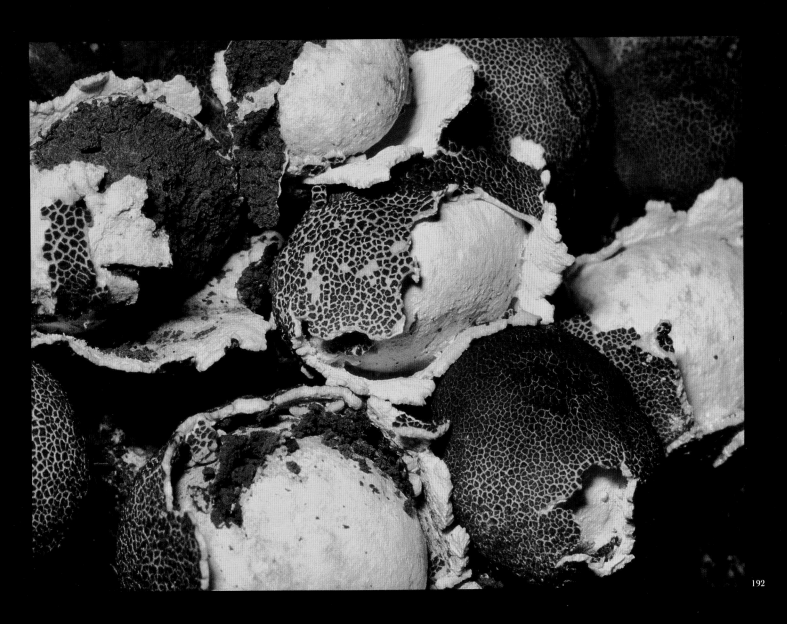

192

**192  YELLOW EARTHBALL FUNGUS, COSTA RICA** (Michael and Patricia Fogden)
CERTAIN FUNGI GROW ONLY ON CERTAIN MATERIALS, WHICH THEY BREAK DOWN
AS THEY FEED ON THEM. THE PARASOL FUNGI (191) SEEM TO GROW MAINLY ON
DEAD LEAVES; THESE EARTHBALLS, ALTHOUGH THEY APPEAR TO EMERGE
DIRECTLY FROM THE SOIL, GROW ON SPECIFIC KINDS OF DEAD WOOD.

194

193

195

**193  STINKHORN, UNDESCRIBED SPECIES, COSTA RICA** (Michael and Patricia Fogden)

**194  FUNGUS IN CLOUD FOREST, EAST AFRICA** (Peter Ward/Bruce Coleman Ltd)

**195  FUNGUS, SABAH** (Ivan Polunin/NHPA)

FUNGI PRODUCE REPRODUCTIVE SPORES WHICH NEED TO BE DISPERSED AND,
LIKE MANY GREEN PLANTS, THEY SOMETIMES ENLIST THE HELP OF INSECTS. THE
STINKHORN PRODUCES AN UNPLEASANT-SMELLING LIQUID ATTRACTIVE TO FLIES,
WHICH COLLECT SPORES ON THEIR FEET TO SCATTER ELSEWHERE; OTHER FUNGI
EXPLODE, SCATTERING THEIR DUST-LIKE SPORES AROUND THEM. STILL OTHERS
IMPREGNATE INSECTS WHICH MOVE ON AND THEN DIE, PROVIDING NUTRITION
FOR THE FUNGI WHICH GROW FROM THEIR BODIES AND WHICH THEN SCATTER
THEIR SPORES ONTO YET MORE UNWITTING INSECTS.

**196  TERMITE WORKERS HARVESTING DEAD LEAVES, MALAYSIA**
(Ken Preston-Mafham/Premaphotos)
THERE ARE ABOUT 2000 SPECIES OF TERMITES THROUGHOUT THE FORESTS OF
THE WORLD, ALL SHYING AWAY FROM LIGHT AND DROUGHT, LIVING IN
ELABORATE MUD MOUNDS OR UNDERGROUND NESTS. THEY ARE IMPORTANT
DECOMPOSERS OF PLANT MATTER, CLEANING THE FOREST BY VORACIOUSLY
FEEDING ON DEAD WOOD DIGESTED WITH THE HELP OF MICRO-ORGANISMS
LIVING IN THEIR GUT.

197

**197  NYMPHALID BUTTERFLY
FEEDING ON DUNG, PERU**
(Ken Preston-Mafham/Premaphotos
MANY BUTTERFLIES FEED ON
ANIMAL WASTE SUCH AS URINE
AND DUNG, SUPPLEMENTING THE
SALT WHICH IS LOST IN SPERM
PRODUCTION IN PARTICULAR.
THEY, TOO, HELP TO RECYCLE
NUTRIENTS WHICH MIGHT
OTHERWISE BE DISSOLVED BY THE
RAIN AND LOST.

**198  FORAGING ARMY ANTS,
TRINIDAD**
(David Thompson/OSF)
RAINFOREST ANTS ARE
CARRION-EATERS AS WELL AS
BEING PREDATORS OF LIVING
INSECTS. THEY CAN QUICKLY
DISMEMBER ANY CARCASS THEY
FIND ON THE FOREST FLOOR. THE
HOOK-LIKE JAWS OF THESE ARMY
ANTS ARE SO STRONG THAT THEY
WERE USED BY AMERICAN INDIANS
TO 'STITCH' WOUNDS: THE ANT WAS
MADE TO BITE EITHER SIDE OF THE
CUT, DRAWING THE SKIN
TOGETHER: ITS BODY WAS THEN
REMOVED, LEAVING ONLY THE
JAWS.

198

*CHAPTER NINE*

# PEOPLE OF THE FOREST
## Robin Hanbury-Tenison

*If you damage your environment, it will no longer support your needs. This simple but essential rule is unwittingly complied with by all the creatures of the animal kingdom. Ironically, the human race all too often ignores it. The consequences can be dire. But in many of the ancient tropical rainforests live people who do understand the imperative of maintaining the finely balanced ecosystem on which they depend for all they need. Over the millennia, forest peoples have found ever more sophisticated methods of simultaneously exploiting and managing their environment, acknowledging their debt to the land in a multitude of ways. We might well follow their example, and learn from their great expertise: but the chances of doing so are fast disappearing. For the people of the rainforest, discounted and exploited in the race for financial gain, are losing their cultural identities, their freedom and even their lives with every acre of forest destroyed.*

The rainforests were already many millions of years old when the first hunter-gatherers ventured into their vast and unknown interior. The forests of South East Asia were the first to be colonized, some forty thousand years ago; much later, people also entered those of America and Africa. Travelling nomadically, the ancestral pioneers probably carried few possessions besides their intelligence and resourcefulness. As they migrated ever deeper into the forest, they began to discover how best to extract a living from the world which towered around them.

Since those first hunter-gatherers began to learn which fruits were the sweetest and which game the best, which vines healed wounds and which yielded lethal arrow poison, such forest lore

---

**199  CHIEF RAONI, BRAZIL** (Bill Leimbach/South American Pictures)
RAONI, A CHIEF OF THE KAYAPO INDIANS IN XINGU, BRAZIL, HAS BECOME A SYMBOL OF THE WORLDWIDE STRUGGLE TO SAVE THE TROPICAL RAINFORESTS. FOR THOUSANDS OF YEARS, RAONI'S ANCESTORS HAVE LIVED IN THE FOREST; IT HAS SUPPLIED THEIR EVERY NEED AND HAS, IN RETURN, BEEN TREATED WITH GREAT REVERENCE. TODAY, HIS PEOPLE SEE HUGE TRACTS OF THEIR TERRITORY QUITE LITERALLY GOING UP IN SMOKE TO MAKE WAY FOR RANCHING, MINING, AND FARMING: SUCH AREAS WILL PROBABLY NEVER AGAIN BE ABLE TO SUPPORT RAINFOREST GROWTH. WITH THE LOSS OF THEIR LANDS, FOREST PEOPLE EVERYWHERE ARE LOSING THEIR VERY MEANS OF SURVIVAL, ALONG WITH THEIR EXTRAORDINARY CULTURES, REFINED OVER THE MILLENNIA TO ENABLE THEM TO LIVE IN BALANCE WITH THE MOST COMPLEX NATURAL ENVIRONMENTS ON EARTH.

has been passed down by their descendants through the generations. Over the centuries it has accumulated, and today, the few traditional forest peoples which remain – there are about a thousand tribes scattered through Central Africa, South America and South East Asia – are unrivalled in their understanding of that most complex of ecosystems, the rainforest: their home.

Such an understanding has given rise to cultures governed above all by an awareness of the debt owed to the forest, which supplies all the essentials of life: food, shelter, tools, medicines and so on. It return it is treated with immense respect, even deified; to abuse it may be regarded as a crime. We should not, however, cast too romantic a light on the forest people, whose life is often far from idyllic: their reasons for adopting a non-destructive lifestyle are highly practical. With a foresight which is sadly lacking in our own society and disastrously ignored by those who are at this very moment bulldozing their way through the trees, the people of the forest know and appreciate only too well that if you destroy your environment, it will no longer fulfil your needs.

This simple but essential principle is enshrined in every aspect of the life of rainforest peoples, one example being the Yanomami Indians of the Amazon rainforests. The largest un-acculturated tribe in all the Americas, the Yanomami are a proud people with an intense spiritual life, in which they are led by their Shaman, the healer-mystic common to many tribal societies. Although they reap rich rewards from hunting and gathering, the Yanomami also obtain much of their food from agriculture, but – remarkably in the rainforest, where the already impoverished soils generally become barren after a few years of farming – an agriculture which does not leave the land a desert.

Deep in the forest, the Yanomami clear small areas in which are planted a great range of crops with uses ranging from food to medicine to magic. In their tangled variety the Yanomami's gardens imitate the diversity of the forest, mimicking the conditions of the natural ecosystem. In this way, the animals essential for the forest's reproduction are maintained; palms and shrubs of varying height protect others beneath them from the desiccating tropical sun, and are shaded in turn by the tall trees around the clearing; while the range of plants and the binding roots of the tree stumps which are left help to retain the soil's nutrients. This is 'agroforestry' in essence, the basis on which scientists are now developing methods for sustainable agriculture in the tropics.

Such small clearings are quickly re-seeded by surrounding trees and other plants: the Yanomami allow their gardens to become overgrown almost as soon as they are cleared, but continue to work them for several years before moving to a new, more fertile site. Undisturbed, the forest regenerates and the soil regains its health; within a decade or so the gardens are un-recognizable. Only the Yanomami know where they used to farm, and will return for up to fifty years to harvest, say, the fruits of a peach palm in areas which already contain sturdy young trees; for such small-scale disturbance can actually be beneficial to the ecosystem. This is forest management at its most successful: it is far removed from the mass clearance which is now so widespread, and from which the land can never recover.

There are many examples of such subtle environmental management among forest people. It has taken years for West-ern scientists to appreciate the importance of inter-species re-lationships to the forest ecosystem: the nomadic hunter-gatherer Penan people of Borneo, however, have long under-stood them, and even taken measures to conserve them. They are particularly careful not to overcull the bearded pigs whose herds they follow, and likewise do not fell certain trees, in-cluding the mighty dipterocarps which, to the horror of the Penan, fall all too often to the chainsaws of the logging com-panies. The Penan do not fell the trees because the pigs depend on their fruits for food, and they do not kill too many pigs because, in turn, the trees depend on them to disperse their seeds. If they destroyed one, the other would suffer – and so, ultimately, would the Penan.

A nomadic lifestyle like that of the Penan both maximizes access to the forest's resources while limiting the damage caused by exploiting them. The Baka of Cameroon in Central Africa are also traditionally nomadic, though they now spend over half the year in permanent villages, still taking most of what they need from the forest. Their semi-sedentary lifestyle is not a recent symptom of acculturation (as it often is for tradi-tionally nomadic people) but an arrangement which is probably centuries old, enabling them to work in the plantations of neighbouring villages in exchange for the goods they need but cannot make.

The Baka are one of several groups of the people known as Pygmies (they dislike the name) who live in the forests of Central Africa, in extended family groups of perhaps thirty in-dividuals. Gentle and humorous, they have little organized hierarchy and tend to settle conflicts within the community by ridiculing the protagonists – an extremely judicious method when so much depends on group unity.

Like the Yanomami, the Baka rely to some extent on culti-vated produce for starchy foods in particular, but they are, first and foremost, hunter-gatherers. Towards the end of the dry season, as the harvest of the villagers' coffee and cocoa planta-tions draws to a close and game around the main camp grows scarce, the Baka become restless. Finally, they leave for the deep forest. Here they live entirely in the old manner, travelling in small groups, their few possessions laden into the women's baskets, drawing on each area they pass through for what it can offer: game, fish, mushrooms, yams, fruits or insects.

Superbly skilful in the ways of the forest, the Baka 'read' the signs which will lead them to find food: a few faint tracks, a mound of half-eaten fruits, the shaking of leaves in the treetops, the call of a certain bird or the flowering of a certain tree. They can tell, for instance, by the flight path of a bee or even its buzzing high in the canopy where its nest is located: later they will scale the tree, despite its dizzying height, to plunder the nest for the honeycombs it contains.

As they move through the forest, the Baka build small hunting camps, clearing a small area but leaving the large trees – for, environmental considerations aside, these would take hours to fell. The women weave igloo-shaped huts from pliable saplings and thatch them with large leaves, until they become organic mounds in the shifting, dappled light of the understorey. At night, there may be a dance or a story by firelight, designed for entertainment but also to celebrate the forest and weaken the animals for the hunters. After a few days, the group moves on. A week later, tendrils curl around the huts of the abandoned camp; on occasion the sapling frameworks actually root and produce new green shoots.

The Baka are motivated to begin their long forest trips by the onset of the rainy season, for this heralds the fruiting of the wild mango trees. Wild mangoes are valued not only for their juicy flesh, but also for the oil-yielding kernel they contain: animals seek out the fruits as well, so game is plentiful and easy to track in the damp ground. An awareness of the seasons and moods of the forest, and how they influence its plants and animals, is central to the lives of such people, allowing them to exploit their environment with supreme efficiency. The Yanomami, for instance, collect more than five hundred different wild plants, as well as fruit, fish, frogs and even insects such as caterpillars and termites at different times during the forest cycle, and their meals are seldom identical on two consecutive days throughout the year.

Among all the diverse life of the forest, only people are able to access every part of their environment – even turning its defences to their own advantage. The early hunter-gatherers must have been avid and adventurous experimenters, for today their descendants know the individual properties of literally thousands of plants: in many varied and extraordinary ways they exploit the chemistry of the forest, often the very chemicals designed by plants to protect themselves from predators. Over the generations, plants have been found to dull pain, heal wounds, cure fever, induce visions, reduce or increase fertility, stimulate or tranquillise; poisons have been found which kill fish or game but are harmless when taken by mouth.

A meagre one per cent of tropical rainforest plants have been investigated by Western scientists for their potential. This is thrown into perspective when we remember that some forty per cent of prescribed drugs have a (mainly tropical) plant origin. Although scientists began to take tribal healers seriously only very recently, many drug-yielding plants were only 'discovered' because of their place in traditional medicine. The dainty, pink-flowered Rosy Periwinkle of Madagascar had been used by forest people for generations: in 1960 its properties were finally investigated. Then, four out of every five children with leukaemia died; today, with drugs derived from the Rosy Periwinkle, the same number now survive.

There are many more examples. Quinine, the first effective and widely used treatment for malaria, is derived from the bark of the South American Chinchona tree. It has now been largely replaced by synthetic drugs, but in the wake of increasing resistance by the malaria parasite to these treatments, scientists are once more turning to the 'fever bark' tree for inspiration. The contraceptive pill is derived from a Mexican yam: many other natural contraceptives (and abortives) are used by forest people. Curare, with which the Amazonian Indians poison-tip their arrows, is the basis of a muscle relaxant now used extensively in Western surgery; while the cardiac glycosides of African Strophanthus vine seeds, also used in making arrow poison, are stimulants which are now used in the treatment of heart disease.

The list goes in, but the important point is that plants, particularly rainforest plants, are sources of an immense range of chemicals. Their uninvestigated potential could yield a still greater range of medicines, not to mention other useful substances – foods, perfumes, insecticides, dyes, waxes, fuels, oils, and hundreds more. Forest people, by definition, know their individual properties better than anyone: but with every acre of forest that is destroyed, the possibilities for new discoveries are reduced. This is partly because the plants themselves are being lost – it has been estimated that one animal or plant becomes extinct every half hour because of environmental abuse – but more particularly because the traditional, unwritten knowledge of forest people is itself rapidly disappearing. The forest people are losing their knowledge along with their culture; and they are losing their culture mainly because its source, the forest, is disappearing.

Knowledge, however, may be the very least of their losses as their world is flattened around them. For the peoples of the forest, the devastation of their homeland spells rapid cultural degeneration, despair and often the death of the whole tribe. In Brazil alone one tribe has become extinct every year since the turn of the century.

Only in this century have other humans appeared in great numbers in the rainforest: but they are destroying it at such a prodigious rate that if they continue, within forty years only isolated pockets of forest will be left. The traditional forest dwellers are powerless to resist as their home is plundered for timber and mineral wealth, and razed to the ground to make way for huge development programmes or cattle ranches so that we in the West can eat a cheaper hamburger. Ironically, vast areas of forest are also now being destroyed by millions of people who may depend on the land as much as the tribal groups, but who have been driven to exploit the forests through overpopulation, the environmental degradation of their own ancestral lands, or political pressure to move to what are seen as virgin territories. Like the Yanomami, these people burn areas of forest to clear it for agriculture, but this method cannot support their numbers and requirements: a wasteland results and the people themselves suffer.

Everywhere, the carefully balanced and sustainable lifestyles of forest people, which have been refined and developed over the centuries, are being devastated. In Borneo, to take just one example, the lives of the sedentary long house people of the great inland rivers are destroyed by logging. The soil washes away once the trees are removed; their life, based on rice growing and forest produce, becomes untenable. The rivers silt up, killing the fish and making navigation difficult, forcing them to abandon their homelands and migrate to coastal towns, where they become a social problem.

Meanwhile the Penan, who nurture their environment so carefully, are simply pushed off their land by the logger's bulldozers. When they protest with passive resistance by forming human chains to block the roads being thrust into their last refuges, they are arrested. Like all nomadic peoples, they do not settle in one place with ease: and yet this is the proposed solution to the problem of the loss of the great spaces which were theirs.

The story is hardly happier in Africa, which has already lost so much of its rainforests. Forestry roads cut gashes through the green; great trees like the mahoganies are felled and dragged out, toppling and splintering many more in their wake. Although a few Baka groups are still untouched by the destruction, all around them their land is disappearing: when it finally goes, their culture will follow. This has already happened to other Pygmy groups in Central Africa: it is supremely ironic that in many places they are employed by the timber companies for a paltry wage, to assist in devastating their own home and with it, all the game, fish, plants and the like which have supported them for millennia.

Perhaps the worst onslaught of all faces the Yanomami. Gold and uranium have been found in the heartland of their territory, and the area has been invaded by 50,000 Brazilians, themselves desperate for a place to live and a chance to find a livelihood, who bring with them guns, disease and destruction. The mercury used to extract the gold is polluting the rivers, killing the fish and making the water unsafe to drink; shanty towns proliferate and the Indians, who have always been fiercely territorial, are hugely outnumbered. Already the Indians have suffered widespread loss of life through what are effectively unofficial eradication programmes – they have been shot, bombed and poisoned, and fallen victim to deliberately introduced diseases to which they have no resistance. Technically, many areas of their land are protected, but in reality, corruption and commercial greed ensure that almost nothing is done about the plight of 'just a few Indians.'

Ironically, the lives of people who are not, strictly speaking 'traditional' forest dwellers, but who have nonetheless exploited their environment without damaging it for generations, can be even more savagely attacked than those of the indigenous inhabitants. The rubber tappers of Brazil – *seringueiros* – do no harm to the wild trees which provide their income and supply one of the most vital products of the industrialized world: but they are now in the way of short-sighted and greedy politicians and land speculators, who see progress in burning down the forest to create ranches. Many *seringueiros* have been murdered in the struggle, notably their charismatic leader Chico Mendes, who received the UNEP Global 500 Award before he was assassinated in 1988.

It is, ultimately, difficult to apportion blame. Most rainforest countries have massive foreign debts, and are keen to obtain currency where they can. Often they perceive their traditional people as savages, who can only impede progress, and the rainforest as a resource which is theirs to do with as they like. But what of the financial stranglehold exerted by the Western banks who supply the loans, and what of foreign investment in rainforest exploitation; and what of the track record of Western countries – we who destroyed so much of our own forest so long ago?

At long last, however, the realisation is dawning that the destruction of rainforests is not only local in effect, but has world-wide repercussions. That the gains from removing forest are short term and often illusory, and that for the trouble-torn tropical countries, the real key to an economically sound future must partly lie in properly managing, rather than simply looting, the environment. It is even beginning to be appreciated that the ancient forests could be their most precious assets, holding many a valuable resource which could be extracted on a sustainable, long-lasting basis.

It would be only sensible to do so by consulting the people who have lived there for thousands of years, and who understand it so much better than we ever will – as even the best of our ecologists are the first to admit. To exploit the riches of the forest and yet sustain it, we need the help of the experts. This, surely is reason enough to protect their lives and land, even without the moral responsibility we bear to our fellow human beings.

Time is running out very fast. A massive and worldwide shift in perception is needed if we are to halt the process of rainforest destruction. If we could make such a shift, we will all benefit: and where better to start than by heeding the message of the forest peoples. From the Americas to Africa and South East Asia, they share the same conviction: 'We belong to the land' they say, 'not the land to us'.

**200   ALIME, FOUR-YEAR OLD BAKA PYGMY BOY, CAMEROON**
(Lisa Silcock/Dja River Films)

SINCE THE DAY HE WAS BORN, THE ONLY WORLD THIS LITTLE BOY HAS EVER KNOWN HAS BEEN THE FOREST, WHERE THE SUN DOES NOT SET ON THE HORIZON BUT DISAPPEARS OVER THE TREE TOPS, AND A ROAD IS A NARROW TRAIL WHICH WINDS THROUGH THE TREES. THE FOREST, HIS HOME, SUPPLIES HIM WITH ALL HE NEEDS: HIS PARENTS BRING HIM FOOD FROM THE FOREST AND TREAT HIM WITH PLANT MEDICINES WHEN HE IS ILL, WHILE HIS HOUSE IS A SMALL HUT THATCHED WITH LEAVES. AS HE GROWS UP, HE WILL LEARN ABOUT THE WAYS OF THE FOREST, AS ALL BAKA HAVE DONE BEFORE HIM. BUT WILL HIS WORLD REMAIN THE ONE HIS ANCESTORS KNEW, OR DOES HE FACE A VERY DIFFERENT FUTURE?

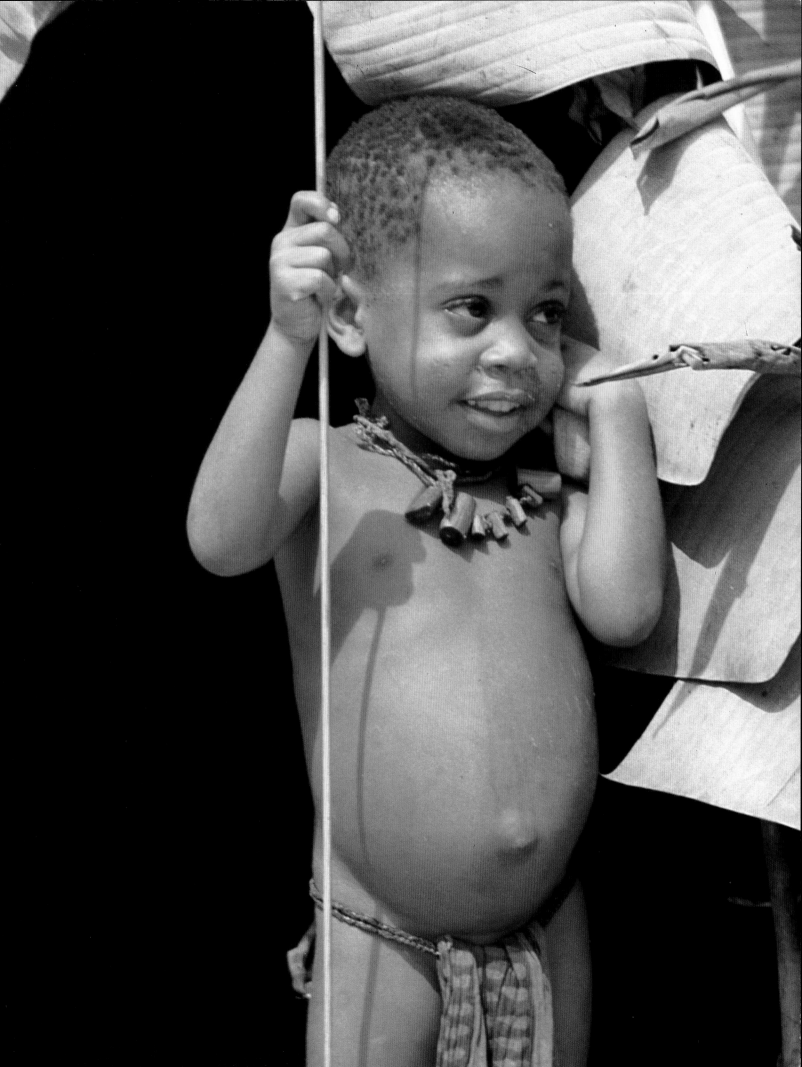

201

**201 ORANG ASLI VILLAGE, PENINSULAR MALAYSIA** (Neil Gale)

**202 BAKA PYGMY VILLAGE, CAMEROON** (Phil Agland/Dja River Films)

**203 OROKO VILLAGE, CAMEROON** (Edward Parker/Hutchison Library)
SINCE THEY FIRST COLONIZED THE RAINFORESTS THOUSANDS OF YEARS AGO,
PEOPLE HAVE FOUND WAYS OF EXTRACTING EVERYTHING THEY NEED FROM
THEIR ENVIRONMENT; BUT, RECOGNIZING THAT IT IS THE KEY TO THEIR
SURVIVAL, THEY HAVE EVOLVED WAYS OF EXPLOITING IT WITHOUT HARMING IT.
EVEN THESE VILLAGE CLEARINGS ARE SMALL ENOUGH TO BE QUICKLY
RECLAIMED BY THE TREES WHEN THE INHABITANTS SHIFT SITES, WHICH THEY
WILL PROBABLY DO AFTER A FEW YEARS. WE COULD LEARN MUCH ABOUT THE
SUSTAINABLE USE OF THE ENVIRONMENT FROM SUCH PEOPLE, IF ONLY THEY
AND THEIR LAND ARE ALLOWED TO SURVIVE.

**204   YANOMAMI INDIANS, BRAZIL**
(Robin Hanbury-Tenison/Robert Harding
Picture Library)
RAINFOREST COMMUNITIES TEND
TO BE SMALL, WHICH BOTH
ENSURES THAT THERE ARE
ENOUGH OF THE FOREST'S
RELATIVELY SCARCE RESOURCES
TO GO ROUND, AND THAT THE
IMPACT OF EACH GROUP ON THE
ENVIRONMENT IS MINIMAL. WHOLE
VILLAGES ARE OFTEN MADE UP OF
A SINGLE MUCH EXTENDED
FAMILY, WHICH ENCOURAGES
HARMONY BETWEEN INDIVIDUALS.
THIS IS IMPORTANT, AS MANY SUCH
SOCIETIES RELY HEAVILY ON
COOPERATION BETWEEN THEIR
MEMBERS. ESSENTIAL JOBS LIKE
HUNTING, GATHERING, FOOD
PREPARATION AND SO ON ALL
TEND TO BE SHARED, THOUGH AS
MUCH FOR THE SAKE OF
COMPANIONSHIP AS EFFICIENCY.

205

**205   YANOMAMI SHAMAN PREPARING HALLUCINOGENIC SNUFF, BRAZIL**

(Robin Hanbury-Tenison/Robert Harding Picture Library)

MOST TRADITIONAL RAINFOREST SOCIETIES IDENTIFY THOUSANDS OF USEFUL
PLANTS, MANY OF WHICH MAY BE USED FOR MEDICAL OR RITUAL PURPOSES. THE
SHAMAN, THE MYSTIC HEALER OF INDIAN SOCIETIES, IS SEEN HERE PREPARING
HALLUCINOGENIC SNUFF FROM THE BARK OF THE VIROLA TREE WHICH WILL
ENABLE HIM TO COMMUNICATE WITH THE YANOMAMI SPIRIT WORLD. IT IS
LIKELY THAT SUCH DRUGS COULD PROVE USEFUL IN TREATING PSYCHOLOGICAL
AND STRESS-RELATED DISORDERS, BUT UNTIL RECENTLY SO LITTLE CREDIT HAS
BEEN GIVEN TO TRADITIONAL MEDICINES THAT VIRTUALLY NONE HAVE BEEN
SCIENTIFICALLY INVESTIGATED. SOME THAT HAVE BEEN ARE NOW USED IN THE
WEST, AND MANY SAVE LIVES. THE FOREST PEOPLE'S KNOWLEDGE COULD REVEAL
THOUSANDS MORE REVOLUTIONARY DRUGS FROM SOURCES AS YET UNKNOWN
TO THE REST OF THE WORLD.

206

207

**206 HEALING WITH FIRE AMONG THE BAKA PYGMIES, CAMEROON**
(Lisa Silcock/Dja River Films)

**207 MOTHER AND FATHER MOURNING DEAD SON, PAPUA NEW GUINEA** (Maureen Mackenzie/Robert Harding Picture Library)
THE OVERLAP BETWEEN THE PHYSICAL AND THE PSYCHOLOGICAL AND SPIRITUAL IS GENERALLY FAR GREATER IN TRADITIONAL SOCIETIES THAN IN OUR OWN. ILLNESS MAY OFTEN BE ATTRIBUTED TO BAD SPIRITS OR ILL-WISHERS; HENCE THE USE OF MAGIC AND RITUAL – AS IN THE FIRE CEREMONY (206) – TO HEAL. AN AWARENESS OF THE SPIRIT WORLD IS EXTREMELY IMPORTANT: A DEATH IS OFTEN ACCOMPANIED BY SPECIFIC MOURNING RITUALS, WHICH ARE DESIGNED TO APPEASE THE SPIRIT OF THE DECEASED, ENSURING THAT IT RESTS QUIETLY AND DOES NOT DISTURB THE LIVING.

208

**208 YANOMAMI WOMEN
COLLECTING FIREWOOD, BRAZIL**
(Robin Hanbury-Tenison/Robert Harding
Picture Library)
IT MAY SEEM NO DIFFICULT TASK
TO COLLECT FIREWOOD WHEN YOU
ARE SURROUNDED BY TREES, BUT
EVEN IN SUCH SIMPLE JOBS, AS IN
ALL ASPECTS OF FOREST LIFE,
SOME SPECIALIZED KNOWLEDGE IS
NEEDED, WHICH COMES FROM
LESSONS LEARNED IN CHILDHOOD.
SOME WOODS BURN THROUGH THE
NIGHT, OTHERS FLARE AND
QUICKLY DIE; WHILE DAMP WOOD
AND NEW WOOD DO NOT BURN AT
ALL.

209

210

**209   CLIMBING FOR HONEY, CAMEROON** (Lisa Silcock/Dja River Films)

**210   A HAUL OF WILD HONEYCOMBS, CAMEROON** (Lisa Silcock/Dja River Films)
FOR THE BAKA PYGMIES OF CAMEROON, HONEY IS THE MOST PRIZED FOOD OF
ALL: THEY COLLECT IT FROM SEVENTEEN DIFFERENT KINDS OF BEE USING A
VARIETY OF TECHNIQUES. THE AFRICAN HONEYBEE NESTS HIGH IN THE CANOPY.
A SKILLED CLIMBER WILL SCALE THE TRUNK WITH THE AID OF A BELT MADE
FROM LIANAS AS HIS ONLY SUPPORT (209), IN ORDER TO REACH THE DRIPPING
GOLDEN COMBS (210). THE RISK, THEY CONSIDER, IS WORTH IT, FOR THESE NESTS
CAN YIELD 9KG/20LB OF HONEY DURING THE FOREST'S PEAK FLOWERING SEASON.

211

**211 BAKA WOMEN IN PLANTATION, CAMEROON**
(Lisa Silcock/Dja River Films)
ALTHOUGH THEY WERE ORIGINALLY COMPLETELY NOMADIC HUNTERS AND GATHERERS, IT IS PROBABLY SEVERAL CENTURIES SINCE THE BAKA BECAME SEMI-SETTLED AND BEGAN TO SUPPLEMENT THEIR DIET WITH CULTIVATED FOODS. STARCHY FOODS ARE PARTICULARLY SCARCE IN THE FOREST, SO THE CARBOHYDRATE OFFERED BY PLANTAINS, MANIOC AND THE LIKE IS HIGHLY DESIRABLE. SUCH FOODS ARE OFTEN GIVEN TO THE BAKA BY NEIGHBOURING VILLAGERS IN EXCHANGE FOR A DAY'S WORK; HOWEVER, SOME BAKA GROUPS NOW HAVE THEIR OWN PLANTATIONS, WHICH GIVES THEM FAR GREATER INDEPENDENCE.

**212 YANOMAMI IN PLANTATION, BRAZIL** (Peter Frey/Survival International)
THE YANOMAMI HUNT AND GATHER FOREST PRODUCE BUT ARE ALSO EXCELLENT SMALL-SCALE AGRICULTURALISTS. THEY CLEAR SMALL 'GARDENS' IN THE FOREST WHICH THEY PLANT WITH A HUGE VARIETY OF CROPS, INCLUDING PLANTAINS, MANIOC, PEACH PALMS, PAPAYA TREES, SUGAR CANE AND MAIZE. THEY ALSO CULTIVATE NON-FOOD PLANTS SUCH AS COTTON, MEDICINAL AND MAGIC PLANTS, HUNTING POISONS, AND OTHERS WHICH ARE MADE INTO ROPE AND ARROWS. NO ATTEMPT IS MADE TO PREVENT THESE GARDENS FROM BECOMING OVERGROWN: THEY ARE QUICKLY RECOLONIZED BY SEEDS FROM SURROUNDING TREES AND HAVE NO HARMFUL IMPACT ON THE FOREST.

212

**213 BAKA PREPARING ARROW POISON, CAMEROON**
(Lisa Silcock/Dja River Films)
PEOPLE FROM RAINFORESTS ALL OVER THE WORLD USE PLANT POISONS IN HUNTING, OFTEN EXPLOITING THE VERY COMPOUNDS THE PLANT HAS EVOLVED TO PROTECT. ITSELF FROM PREDATORS. THE BAKA USE THE CRUSHED SEEDS OF A STROPHANTHUS VINE MIXED WITH OTHER PLANTS TO TIP THEIR CROSSBOW ARROWS. THE VINE CONTAINS STROPHANTHINE, A POTENT CARDIAC POISON WHICH IS USED IN WESTERN MEDICINE IN THE TREATMENT OF HEART DISEASE.

213

**214 PENAN HUNTER USING A BLOW GUN, BORNEO** (C. & B. Leimbach/Robert Harding Picture Library)
THE SKILL OF BLOW GUN HUNTERS IS WELL DOCUMENTED, BUT THE FORCE OF THE ARROW ALONE WOULD BE INEFFECTIVE ON ALL BUT THE SMALLEST PREY. HOWEVER, EVEN A SLIGHT PUNCTURE BY A POISON-TIPPED DART IS ENOUGH TO KILL A LARGE ANIMAL: MONKEYS IN PARTICULAR ARE HUNTED IN THIS WAY. THE POISON ENTERS THE BLOODSTREAM, ARRESTING HEART FUNCTION WITHIN JUST A FEW MINUTES.

214

**215  INDIANS WITH MONKEYS, ECUADOR**

(John Wright/Hutchison Library)
THE MIRACLE OF HUNTING POISONS IS THAT THEY ARE INEFFECTIVE WHEN TAKEN BY MOUTH, SO THE MEAT IS QUITE SAFE TO EAT. RAINFOREST-DWELLING PEOPLES HAVE ACCUMULATED THEIR IMPRESSIVE AND USEFUL KNOWLEDGE OF PLANT PROPERTIES OVER A VERY LONG TIME. THIS INFORMATION IS POTENTIALLY EXTREMELY VALUABLE, EVEN LUCRATIVE – WHICH SHOULD ENCOURAGE EVEN THE MOST MERCENARY OF GOVERNMENTS TO SEE THE RAINFORESTS AS A RESOURCE TO BE PROTECTED.

215

216

217

**216 BAKA FAMILY SHARING GAME, CAMEROON**

(Lisa Silcock/Dja River Films)
MEAT IS PRIZED AMONG ALL HUNTER-GATHERERS, AND RANKS IN IMPORTANCE FAR ABOVE VEGETABLE FOODS. AS WELL AS HUNTING WITH POISON-TIPPED ARROWS AND CROSSBOWS, THE BAKA USE LONG SPEARS AND ALSO SET TRAPS, THOUGH THIS IS A BORROWED TECHNIQUE. THEY ARE EXTREMELY SKILLED TRACKERS WHO CAN IDENTIFY AND HUNT DOWN AN ANIMAL GUIDED ONLY BY THE FAINTEST HOOFPRINT, THE SLIGHTEST SOUND, OR THE CRUSHED VEGETATION WHICH INDICATES ITS PATH.

218

**217 GRILLING YAMS, PAPUA NEW GUINEA** (Jack Fields/ZEFA)
YAMS ARE THE MAIN WILD SOURCE OF STARCH FOUND IN THE WILD: THEY TASTE BETTER BUT REQUIRE MUCH MORE EFFORT TO PROCURE THAN CULTIVATED FOODS.

**218 EDIBLE BEETLE LARVAE, CAMEROON**

(Lisa Silcock/Dja River Films)
SURPRISINGLY, PROTEIN IS NOT ALWAYS EASY TO COME BY IN THE FOREST: AT CERTAIN TIMES OF YEAR GAME IS SCARCE AND THE NUMBERS OF FISH, CRABS AND SHRIMPS DWINDLE. EDIBLE CATERPILLARS AND BEETLE LARVAE THEN PROVIDE AN ALTERNATIVE WHICH MAY SEEM REPELLENT TO US, BUT WHICH IS HIGHLY NUTRITIOUS.

219

**219  WOMAN WEARING
TRADITIONAL FACE PAINT, PAPUA
NEW GUINEA** (Mike McCoy/OSF)

**220  APPLYING FACE PAINT, PAPUA
NEW GUINEA** (Maureen Mackenzie/
Robert Harding Picture Library)

220

**221   CHILD IN RITUAL PAINT OF CLOSING CEREMONY, PAPUA NEW GUINEA** (Maureen Mackenzie/Robert Harding Picture Library)
DECORATION IS USED BY PEOPLE EVERYWHERE, BUT THE PAPUA NEW GUINEANS ARE MASTERS OF THE ART. THESE INTRICATE PATTERNS, WHICH CONTAIN BOTH ELEMENTS OF SPIRITUAL BELIEF AND REFERENCES TO THE NATURAL WORLD, ARE NOT JUST FOR EFFECT BUT ARE HIGHLY RITUALIZED AND USED ACCORDING TO STRICT RULES. SUCH SKILLS AND TRADITIONS, LIKE THE EXTENSIVE BUT UNWRITTEN KNOWLEDGE HELD BY THE FOREST PEOPLE, ARE PASSED DOWN ORALLY AND BY EXAMPLE THROUGH THE GENERATIONS. HEREIN LIES THEIR VULNERABILITY: CULTURAL KNOWLEDGE CAN DISAPPEAR ALL TOO EASILY FROM THE WORLD WHEN UNRECORDED, PARTICULARLY WHEN HELD BY A DISREGARDED MINORITY. THOUSANDS AND THOUSANDS OF FOREST PEOPLE HAVE ALREADY LOST THEIR LANDS AND CULTURAL IDENTITY, AND WITH THEM MANY CENTURIES OF ACCUMULATED LEARNING. THE WELFARE OF SUCH PEOPLE SHOULD BE PROTECTED ON COMPASSIONATE GROUNDS ALONE, BUT ALSO FOR THE SAKE OF THE FUTURE: FOR THE PEOPLE OF THE RAINFOREST MAY HOLD THE KEY TO A DIFFERENT, AND BETTER, WORLD FOR US ALL.

*CONCLUSION*
# FUTURE IN THE BALANCE
### ROGER HAMMOND

FOR MILLIONS OF YEARS, THE RAINFORESTS OF THE WORLD HAVE EXISTED relatively undisturbed. Their myriad animals and plants have evolved in response to their environment and to each other and generations of traditional rainforest people have survived by learning to live with their environment.

During the last century another culture has entered the forest: a culture driven by a pernicious cycle of growth and expansion. Natural checks against over-exploitation have been confounded because those who are now consuming the products of the forest are not those who experience the immediate effects of its degradation. There are millions who do, however, and it is now understood that in the short term the disappearance of rainforests will threaten the lives of over one billion people, as their water resources dry up and their land turns to dust. Many of these people actually live in the forests themselves and are utterly dependent on them. In the longer term this destruction may change the world's climate and therefore the history of the planet.

Pressures on our remaining forests are intense and it would be foolish to expect that all remaining forest can be protected. When environmental organizations work with governments to establish national parks and protected areas, it is vital to take account of the economic forces which impel people and institutions to abuse forests.

In principle there is much that can be done to satisfy the need to generate income whilst protecting the rainforests. Farmers can be taught new and more productive ways of using land and, if population growth can be controlled, a stable forest system can be the result. Tropical plantations may be rationalized through agroforestry so that they are economically and ecologically appropriate. Combinations of species may be grown which will provide higher and more sustainable income levels. Forest management can be reformed to relate harvests of logs to tree growth and regeneration rates. The nature of the harvest can be diversified to take account of outputs other than timber through the development of extractive reserves. Reserves for genetic resources can be paid for through royalties on existing forest products.

Knowledge and capital are needed to help develop farming systems and systems of integrated land use, systems which will result in long term and sustainable income both for individuals and for governments in countries which still retain intact rainforest.

Today, as we enter the last decade of the twentieth century, we have reached a turning point; we can no longer use the excuse of ignorance. We can now make informed decisions about the load we choose to place on our environment: decisions which we know will have an impact for years to come. Are we content to experiment with the loss for all time of a million or more species? Are we satisfied with the prospect of our climate being changed through our apparently insatiable demand for energy? Early this century Albert Einstein asserted that God did not play dice with the universe. Now, at the end of that century, are we prepared to gamble with the earth?

---

CRACKED AND USELESS EARTH – THE RESULTS OF MINING IN A FORMER
RAINFOREST AREA, BRAZIL
(Steve Bowles)

# THE LIVING EARTH FOUNDATION

L IVING EARTH IS ONE OF A NUMBER OF ORGANIZATIONS working internationally to help bring about change. The human being has the unique quality of being able to look forward in time. Our governments must learn to be responsible for the future, just as individuals must learn to be responsible to future generations.

In buying this book you have helped to fund our work in West Africa, specifically with an education programme in Cameroon which will be funded with the help of the royalties earned by this book. The rainforest in Cameroon is threatened, as is all rainforest, but there the government has welcomed the assistance of Living Earth on a programme of education which is helping a growing generation to learn more of their inheritance and to develop the means which will ensure a future for their forest.

Half the funding for this project has been provided by the British Government's Overseas Development Administration. This funding is contingent on Living Earth raising an equivalent amount, which is derived from donations from the public and through partnerships with the business sector. If you wish to know more about the work of Living Earth further information can be obtained from our UK office.

Living Earth Foundation
Registered charity number 800672

# ORGANIZATIONS INVOLVED IN TROPICAL RAINFOREST CONSERVATION

*The following conservation organizations have a particular interest in tropical rainforest conservation, working on local, national and international levels, through research, education and a variety of activities to increase world awareness.*

ACTION FOR ENVIRONMENT
PO Box 10-030
Wellington
New Zealand

THE ARK TRUST
500 Harrow Road
London W9 3QA
England

AUSTRALIAN CONSERVATION
FOUNDATION
672b Glenferrie Road
Hawthorn Vic 3122
Australia

CAMPAIGN TO SAVE NATIVE
FORESTS
794 Hay Street
Perth W.A. 6000
Australia

COMPANIA NACIONAL DE
REFORESTACION (CONARE)
Apartado Postal 17015
El Conde
Caracas 1010A
Venezuela

CONSERVATION COUNCIL OF
VICTORIA
247 Flinders Lane
Melbourne Vic 3000
Australia

CONSERVATION FOUNDATION
1 Kensington Gore
London SW7 2AR
England

CONSERVATION FOUNDATION
1250 24th Street N.W.
Suite 500
Washington D.C.
20037
United States of America

CONSERVATION INTERNATIONAL
1015 18th St. N.W.
Suite 1002
Washington D.C. 20005
United States of America

CONSERVATION NEW ZEALAND
PO Box 12.200
Wellington
New Zealand

DEPARTMENT OF CONSERVATION
PO Box 10-420
Wellington
New Zealand

EARTHWATCH (EUROPE)
P.O. Box 392
Headington
Oxford
OX3 0UE

ENVIRONMENT &
CONSERVATION ORGANISATION
OF NEW ZEALAND INC.
PO Box 11.057
Wellington
New Zealand

ENVIRONMENTAL DEFENCE
FUND
1616 P Street N.W.
Suite 150
Washington D.C.
20036
United States of America

FAUNA AND FLORA
PRESERVATION SOCIETY
79-83 North Street
Brighton
Sussex
BN1 12A
England

FOREST RESEARCH INSTITUTE
P.O. Box 201
52109 Kuala Lumpa
Malaysia

FRIENDS OF THE EARTH
4th floor
56 Foster Street
Surrey Hills
NSW 2010
Australia

FRIENDS OF THE EARTH
(INTERNATIONAL)
530 Seventh Street S.E.
Washington D.C.
20003
United States of America

FRIENDS OF THE EARTH (NZ)
PO Box 39-065
Auckland West
New Zealand

FRIENDS OF THE EARTH (UK)
26-28 Underwood Street
London N1 7JQ
England

GAIA FOUNDATION
18 Well Walk
London NW3 1LD
England

GLOBAL TOMORROW COALITION
1325 G Street, N.W.
Suite 915
Washington D.C. 20036
United States of America

GREENING AUSTRALIA
Block D, Acton House
Cnr Marcus Clarke Street &
Edinburgh Avenue
Acton Act 2600
Australia

INTERNATIONAL INSTITUTE FOR
ENVIRONMENT AND
DEVELOPMENT (IIED)
3 Endsleigh Street
London WC1H 6DD
England

INTERNATIONAL INSTITUTE FOR
ENVIRONMENT AND
DEVELOPMENT (IIED)
1717 Massachusetts Avenue NW
Washington D.C. 20036
United States of America

INTERNATIONAL UNION FOR
THE CONSERVATION OF NATURE
AND NATURAL RESOURCES
Avenue Mont Blanc
1196 Gland
Switzerland

LIVING EARTH
10 Upper Grosvenor Street
London W1X 9PA
England

MEN OF THE TREES
New South Wales
11 Pebbly Hill Road
Cattai NSW 2756
Australia

NATIONAL AUDUBON SOCIETY
645 Pennsylvania Avenue
SE
Washington D.C. 20003
United States of America

NATIONAL EXECUTIVE OF
ACCLIMATISATION SOCIETY
PO Box 22-021
Wellington
New Zealand

NATIONAL PARKS ASSOCIATION
OF NSW
13th floor,
500 George Street
Sydney NSW 2000
Australia

NATIONAL WILDLIFE
FEDERATION
1412 16th Street NW
Washington D.C. 20003
United States of America

NATURAL RESOURCES DEFENCE
COUNCIL
1350 New York Avenue NW
Washington D.C. 20005
United States of America

NATURE CONSERVATION
COUNCIL OF NSW
39 George Street
Sydney NSW 2000
Australia

NATURE CONSERVANCY
1800 North Kent Street
Arlington
Virginia 22209
United States of America

NEW ZEALAND ASSOCIATION
FOR ENVIRONMENTAL
EDUCATION
Mrs Barbara Spurr
"Ivy Cottage"
Ashley Street
Rangiora
New Zealand

NEW ZEALAND ECOLOGICAL
SOCIETY
PO Box 25-178
Christchurch
New Zealand

NEW ZEALAND GEOGRAPHICAL
SOCIETY
Department of Geography
University of Canterbury
Private Bag
Christchurch
New Zealand

NEW ZEALAND INSTITUTE OF
FORESTRY
PO Box 12-314
Thorndon
Wellington
New Zealand

NEW ZEALAND LAND,
DRAINAGE & RIVER BOARDS
ASSOCIATION
PO Box 246
Hamilton
Wellington
New Zealand

RAINFOREST ACTION NETWORK
300 Broadway
Suite 28
San Francisco
California 94009
United States of America

RAINFOREST ALLIANCE
295 Madison Avenue
Suite 1804
New York
New York 10017
United States of America

RAINFOREST CONSERVATION
SOCIETY INC.
19 Colorado Avenue
Bardon Qld 4065
Australia

RAINFOREST FOUNDATION
(FUNDACAO MATA VIRGEN)
38 Riverview Road
Avalon NSW 2107
Australia

RAINFOREST FOUNDATION
(FUNDACAO MATA VIRGEN)
5 Fitzroy Lodge, The Grove
Highgate
London N6 5JU
England

RAINFOREST FOUNDATION
(FUNDACAO MATA VIRGEN)
PO Box 1167 Venice
California 90294
United States of America

RAINFOREST INFORMATION
CENTRE
7 Wotherspoon Street
Lismore NSW 2480
Australia

ROYAL FOREST AND BIRD
PROTECTION SOCIETY OF NEW
ZEALAND INC.
PO Box 631 Wellington
New Zealand

SAVE THE TREES CAMPAIGN
71 Murphy Road
Zillmere QLD 4034
Australia

SIERRA CLUB
730 Polk Street
San Francisco California 94009
United States of America

SITES/SMITHSONIA INSTITUTE
110 Jefferson Avenue SW
Washington D.C. 20560
United States of America

SURVIVAL INTERNATIONAL
310 Edgware Road
London W2 1DY
England

TOTAL ENVIRONMENT CENTRE
INCORPORATED
3rd Floor, Argyle Centre
18 Argyle Street
Sydney NSW 2000
Australia

TROPICAL ECOSYSTEM
RESEARCH AND RESCUE
ALLIANCE
Terra International
Washington D.C. 20036
United States of Amercia

THE WILDERNESS SOCIETY
130 Davey Street
Hobart TAS 7000
Tasmania

WORLD RESOURCES INSTITUTE
1735 New York Avenie NW
Washington D.C. 20006
United States of America

WWF AUSTRALIA
Level 17
St Martins Tower
31 Market Street
Sydney NSW 2000
Australia

WWF CANADA
60 St Clair Avenue East
Suite 201
Toronto, Ontario M4T 1N5
Canada

WWF INTERNATIONAL
Avenue du Mont-Blanc
1196 Gland
Switzerland

WWF MALAYSIA
P.O.Box 10769
50724 Kuala Lumpa
Malaysia

WWF NEW ZEALAND
35 Taranaki Street
P.O. Box 6237
Wellington
New Zealand

WWF SOUTH AFRICA
P.O. Box 456
Stellenbosch 7600
South Africa

WWF UNITED KINGDOM
Panda House
Weyside Park, Godalming
Surrey GU7 1XR
England

WWF UNITED STATES
1250 24th Street NW
Washington D.C. 20037
United States of America

# ACKNOWLEDGEMENTS

*The publishers would like to thank the following individuals and agencies for permission to use their photographs in this book:*

BRUCE COLEMAN LIMITED
17 Windsor Street
Uxbridge
Middlesex UB8 1AB
UK

SUE CUNNINGHAM
56 Chatham Road
Kingston upon Thames
Surrey KT1 3AA
UK

ELLIS WILDLIFE COLLECTION
69 Cranberry Street
Brooklyn Heights
New York 11201
USA

MICHAEL & PATRICIA FOGDEN
Mid Cambushinnie Cottage
Kinbuck
Dunblane
Perthshire FK15 9JU
Scotland
UK

NICK GORDON
Little Erray
Tobermory
Isle of Mull
Scotland

ROBERT HARDING PICTURE
LIBRARY
17A Newman Street
London W1P 3HD
UK

HUTCHINSON LIBRARY
118 Holland Park Avenue
Holland Park
London W11 4UA
UK

LUIZ CLAUDIO MARIGO
Rua Leitao da Cunha 48
302 Laranjeiras
22251 Rio de Janeiro
Brazil

NATURAL HISTORY
NHPA
Little Tye
Ardingly
Sussex RH17 6TB
UK

OXFORD SCIENTIFIC FILMS
(OSF)
Long Hanborough
Oxford OX7 2LD
UK

PARTRIDGE FILMS
38 Mill Lane
London NW6 1NR
UK

KEN PRESTON MAFHAM
Premaphotos
2 Willoughby Close
Kings Coughton
Warwicks B49 5QJ
UK

ROYAL GEOGRAPHICAL SOCIETY
1 Kensington Gore
London SW7 2AR
UK

REMOTE SOURCE
13 Chapter Street
London SW1P 4NY
UK

SOUTH AMERICAN PICTURES
48 Station Road, Woodbridge
Suffolk IP12 4AT
UK

SURVIVAL INTERNATIONAL
310 Edgware Road
London W2 1DY
UK

WELDON TRANNIES
Suite 4, 52 Ourimbah Road
Mosman NSW 2088
Australia

FEMALE GREEN ANOLE ON
HELICONIA, COSTA RICA
(Michael & Patricia Fogden)

# INDEX

*Figures in italics refer to captions. Individual species are indexed under their own name.*

FIRST PAPERBACK EDITION PUBLISHED IN THE UNITED STATES BY CHRONICLE BOOKS IN 1992

FIRST PUBLISHED IN GREAT BRITAIN IN 1989 BY BARRIE & JENKINS, LTD.

LIBRARY OF CONGRESS CATALOGING IN PUBLICATION DATA

THE RAINFORESTS: A CELEBRATION/COMPILED BY THE LIVING EARTH FOUNDATION:EDITED BY LISA SILCOCK; FOREWORD BY H.R.H. THE PRINCE OF WALES.

P.CM.
ISBN 0-87701-790-5
ISBN 0-8118-0155-1 (pbk.)
1. RAIN FOREST ECOLOGY. 2.RAIN FORESTS I. SILCOCK, LISA.
II. LIVING EARTH FOUNDATION.
QH541.5R27R35 1990
508.315'2-DC20

JACKET DESIGN BY W. BRADLEY CROUCH

CONCEIVED AND EDITED: ANNE FURNISS
DESIGNER: DAVID FORDHAM
ASSISTANT DESIGNER: CAROL MCCLEEVE
PICTURE RESEARCH: HELEN GILKS
PRODUCTION: ROBERT K. CHRISTIE
TYPESETTING: SX COMPOSING LTD., RAYLEIGH, ESSEX
COLOR SEPARATIONS: WANDLE GRAPHICS
PRINTED IN SINGAPORE

10 9 8 7 6 5 4 3 2

CHRONICLE BOOKS
275 FIFTH STREET
SAN FRANCISCO, CALIFORNIA 94103